'Steve enabled the TLG senior team to look differently at our approach to communicating, and at who we are and why we exist. His insight into the decision-making of potential supporters through understanding the Centre Brain gave us a fresh perspective and a methodology to redevelop our communications strategy and approach.'

Tim Morfin, CEO, TLG
(a charity working with young people at risk)

'Steve's insights into how the human brain processes information that causes us to act is vital reading for anyone who wants to create compelling communications that are memorable and result in action. These revolutionary ideas are easily understood and backed up with science, so get reading and use these principles to get the results you want.'

Matt Barlow, CEO, CAP
(a charity helping people out of debt)

Steve Adams works with charities and organizations using Centre Brain as the basis for reviewing, changing and achieving lift-off in brand, communication and organizational story.

Steve also runs half- and full-day seminars, offering a general introduction to Centre Brain, with specific application for participants from a range of contexts, charities and organizations. To find out more and register, visit <www.CentreBrainCommunication.com>.

THE
CENTRE
BRAIN

5 prompts to persuasive power

STEVE
ADAMS

First published in Great Britain in 2017

Society for Promoting Christian Knowledge
36 Causton Street
London SW1P 4ST
www.spck.org.uk

British Library Cataloguing-in-Publication Data
A catalogue record for this book is available from the British Library

ISBN 978–0–281–07790–8
eBook ISBN 978–0–281–07791–5

Typeset by Manila Typesetting Company
Printed in Great Britain by Jellyfish CPI

1 3 5 7 9 10 8 6 4 2

eBook by Manila Typesetting Company

Produced on paper from sustainable forests

To Ruth, Aidan, Oscar, Eben and Poppy
'So many ideas, so little time'

The Centre Brain:
unleashing your persuasive power.

Life is like a ten-speed bicycle. Most of us have gears we never
use.

Charles Schulz

The answer is that we are not helpless in the face of our first
impressions. They may bubble up from the unconscious – from
behind a locked door inside of our brain – but just because
something is outside of awareness doesn't mean it is outside of
control.

Malcolm Gladwell

Contents

Acknowledgements

Without learning French on 300 doorsteps in Belgium as part of a student team in 1993, I'm not sure I'd have become aware of my Centre Brain or begun trying to harness it. So sincere thanks go to the people who developed LAMP (Language Acquisition Made Practical), specifically Dr E. Thomas Brewster, and to the good people of Operation Mobilisation and the 'Famous Five' team who made it so much fun!

Without my buddy and general inspiration JB, who invited me to speak to a group of publishers about using Centre Brain principles in their marketing, I wouldn't have connected with Elizabeth Neep of SPCK. Without Elizabeth, who commissioned this book (and provided a brilliant balance of advice, input, questioning and editing), I wouldn't have climbed out of bed at 4 a.m. for months on end to gather all my thinking on the Centre Brain into a book. Without Alexandra McDonald and Sam Richardson, SPCK might well not have boldly explored new terrain, and I wouldn't have had the honour of writing for a 319-year-old publishing house.

Without the friends who challenged, chipped in, cheered me on and even changed their communication styles because of the ideas in this book, my attempt to create a manual of persuasive communication wouldn't have lifted off.

The Centre Brain wouldn't have left the starting blocks without the reflections of many experts (and friends), including a professor at King's College, London; marketing directors in the Netherlands, Paris, London and the USA; a photographer living near the Queen Elizabeth Olympic Park; and a policy adviser at the Cabinet Office. Nor would I have got very far without the input of clients, companies and charities that commissioned me and then moulded their communication styles in response to advice about using the Centre Brain. And then there are the good people who got excited with me: the many, many friends at Tearfund who encouraged me in my thinking; and my parents, Brian and Alison, who taught me that *'If a job's worth doing, it's worth doing well!'* Thank you, all, for engaging with my thoughts about the Centre Brain.

But an even bigger acknowledgement goes to my four adventurous children and my fun, beautiful wife, who have significantly – although sometimes unintentionally – shaped this book. We'll always have too many ideas – but time with you all is, for me, a life well lived.

And the biggest acknowledgement? To God.

UNDERSTAND WHAT YOU HAVE

'If you want truly to understand something, try to change it.'
— KURT LEWIN

'WE KEEP MOVING FORWARD, OPENING NEW DOORS AND DOING NEW THINGS, BECAUSE WE'RE CURIOUS AND CURIOSITY KEEPS LEADING US DOWN NEW PATHS.'

– WALT DISNEY

1 Doors

'I knew at the time that I'd discovered a bit of my brain I'd unknowingly depended on since birth.'

Late January 1993. An 18-year-old British youth stood on the doorstep of a terraced home in a suburban, French-speaking Belgian village. As the doorbell sounded, his pulse rose. An attractive female of a similar age answered the door. They'd never met before, though would later become friends.

Understanding little or no French, the youth recited the simple French sentences he'd spent the past week memorizing. Arriving in the country, he had been given a cassette-playing Walkman (this being the 1990s). His instructions had been simple: listen repeatedly, then memorize and mimic what you hear. Don't try to translate individual words or phrases. Don't refer to a French-to-English dictionary. He knew his script's general message – but no more. He didn't need it.

As he concluded his sentences, the girl paused, smiled and said something he didn't understand. Hers would be the first of around 300 doors he would knock on that week, just like the other five

18-year-olds he shared a house with. As part of the language-learning project they'd signed up to, they'd pored over a map of the village and divided up the streets. By the end of the first month, each had repeated his or her memorized sentences more than 1,200 times, revisiting the same 300 homes with a new memorized and mimicked message each week.

What the British students said – their memorized message – established with homeowners who they were and why they were there: to learn French. But it was little compared to what they were about to discover – about themselves.

DREAMS

It was in my eighth week of being in Belgium – the eighth week of mimicking the same cassette tapes over and over again – that my 18-year-old self first *dreamt* in French. Incredibly, the dream was not about learning French. Rather, French was the language in which events in the dream unfolded. I was actually *thinking* in French.

Unexpected? Yes. At school the teachers had suggested I drop French before GCSEs started (which I did), having struggled so much with it. Yet after eight weeks in Belgium, I was thinking in French and beginning to instinctively speak and understand the language. I knew at the time that I'd discovered a bit of my brain I'd unknowingly depended on since birth, but had never before intentionally or knowingly engaged with.

I was learning the language, I realized, as I'd first learned English: speaking it without fully understanding the words, and using certain stimuli such as pictures which seemed to communicate with a more powerful area of the brain than before. Possibly for the first time in my 18 years, I was consciously harnessing and directing the hugely powerful *subconscious* area of my brain. In this book, we'll call it the Centre Brain; it's a system of brain structures located nearer the brain's centre and, importantly for this book, it's the part that prompts action.

What I realized was that the techniques we were using to learn French in this unusual way were, in fact, *prompting* or attracting the attention of that normally subconscious region of the brain. This excited me – because this was the action centre, the decision area. And if we could identify what prompted it, we could be much more effective in persuading people.

It was recently found that within a piece of brain the size of a grain of salt there are 100 terabytes of storage capacity. That's the equivalent of 25,000 high-definition movies. In one salt-grain sized crumb. Clearly the 'Centre Brain' holds a great deal of power. But unless 18-year-old me had been forced to go door to door, would I have ever consciously known its potential, and worked out *my* potential to harness and use it? You and I are only aware of a small amount of what's happening in our brains right now. When you see a film, you're consciously aware of those 90 minutes, behind which is months – or years – of unseen work. This book is a backstage pass, behind the scenes of what you're aware of, to your subconscious Centre Brain, to the place where action is prompted and your persuasive potential unleashed.

But how do we learn the 'language' that prompts that action-generating Centre Brain area? Although that part of the brain is always active subconsciously, how do we intentionally awaken and mobilize it in others when we're trying to influence and persuade, harnessing it for our specific purposes?

DISCOVERIES

One of the obstacles to consciously harnessing and prompting this power centre of action in yours – and others' – heads is the bilingual nature of our brains. If you've seen the Disney film *Inside Out*, you'll know about Riley, the little girl who has many and varied mini-characters in her head. Each one is responsible for a key area of her personality – anger, hope, happiness and so on.

Brilliantly (and for some, scarily), in your head and mine, there's a similar arrangement: one part of our brains is responsible for reaching conclusions, the other for prompting action. They work together – the conclusions branch (the Outer Brain) advising the action branch (the Centre Brain).

In *Inside Out*, the characters in Riley's head are very different and often struggle to understand one another. It's the same with us: the two parts of our brains are awoken by different languages. And, as I experienced in Belgium, when different languages are spoken but not mutually understood, making things happen becomes difficult. This book introduces the brain's two languages. It reveals that the Centre Brain's action function can only be intentionally harnessed and directed when someone uses the right language, or set of prompts.

In 2004, I visited the Sahel region of West Africa. A satphone was our only connection to home or help while we were there.

And it worked only when the user found the satellite and pointed the phone directly at it. Move your head a few degrees one way or the other, and communication was broken. Speakers or communicators who fail to use the language of the Centre Brain fail to prompt it to action. They may only be a few degrees off but, like the satellite in space, that part of the brain requires a signal it recognizes for it to be activated and directed.

Finding the satellite in space, before using the satphone, meant standing with the device angled in different directions, hoping you'd strike lucky. Persuading someone – or their Centre Brain – to respond can feel like that: make loads of attempts, and hope one strikes lucky. This book narrows it down, revealing what those prompts are.

A PROMISE

As you read on, various things may begin to make sense. Why, for example, some speakers, bloggers and books you've come across connect with you and make you want to respond. And importantly, why others don't.

In communication terms, if you're in an interview trying to persuade someone to employ you; convincing your girlfriend, boyfriend or spouse that you should both go skydiving; telling a story to an audience of sceptics in a way that begins to change their views; or writing a proposal that you hope will be met with a big green light, then allow me to make you a promise: this book won't offer you a one-size-fits-all magic button to press whenever you need to inspire people to action. It will do much, much more. By giving you understanding, it will enable you to *create* the 'magic button' suited to the situation, whenever you need to inspire people.

Imagine for a moment a place where all communication (written and spoken) is effective and action-inspiring. Let's call it 'The Kingdom of Great Communication'. You may know, from techniques you've tried, what it's like to peer longingly through the window but remain an outsider of that kingdom. By allowing you to understand the language, or prompts, that stimulate action, this book gives you the keys to that communication kingdom.

What you do with them is up to you . . .

'NOTHING IN LIFE IS TO BE FEARED; IT IS ONLY TO BE UNDERSTOOD. NOW IS THE TIME TO UNDERSTAND MORE, SO THAT WE MAY FEAR LESS.'

– MARIE CURIE

2 The point is to understand

'If you've felt frustration at not quite being able to persuade, the answer is here: understand the prompts which stir the brain to action.'

My uncle learned an important lesson the hard way: he was at a party, standing in a circle with a group of old friends, when a couple they hadn't seen for years joined them. Spying the lady had a bump, he instinctively reached out and gently hovered his hand over it. 'Congratulations! When's it due?' he asked. All talking ceased as the group awaited the reply. (If ever a man needed a shovel and advice on digging a hole, fast, it was now.) The lady offered an apologetic explanation that she wasn't, in fact, pregnant. Her husband, attempting to ease the silent awkwardness (though I suspect unintentionally adding to it), added, 'Don't worry – it's not the first time that's happened!' My uncle had presumed that what *he* believed to be true would therefore also be true for those he was communicating with.

Becoming a more persuasive 'version' of yourself doesn't start where you instinctively think it does – with what *you* know or think will generate the response you seek. Just as someone at Alcoholics Anonymous begins with acknowledging helplessness, so persuasiveness begins with acknowledging the limits of your own knowledge. The reason this is so important is because persuasiveness happens *outside* you.

IT'S ALL ABOUT THE LANDING

Persuasiveness starts with where your communication will *land*, not where it takes off from. When we flew into La Paz airport, Bolivia, it seemed as if the plane would go off the end of the runway – the normal slowdown after landing was delayed. Because La Paz airport is one of the world's highest, the air is very thin. The oxygen tanks awaiting passengers with altitude sickness testify to this, as does the length of the runway – a staggering 2.5 miles. Before a plane takes off for La Paz, it must be readied for landing: special tyres capable of withstanding such fast, long landings are fitted.

Advertising guru Leo Burnett framed the take-off/landing question like this: 'The space you should be concerned about is not the space on the paper in front of you but the space in the prospect's mind.'[1]

Effective persuasion begins not with systems or methods for 'take-off' (e.g. the importance of a great opener with a statistic and a story). Instead it starts by looking at the landing: where does what you say need to land to prompt action? If you don't shape your communication for landing, it'll be like a plane polished for take-off, but not fitted with the right tyres for the intended destination.

The language of the Centre Brain isn't words. This means that crafting an eloquently worded script, while important, isn't what will make your communication land well or prompt action.

HARNESSING A DREAM

The reason persuasion isn't as natural or instinctive as we think it should be is because the brain region you speak from is called the Outer Brain – where words 'take off' from. But a different language prompts the brain region where your communication 'lands' – the Centre Brain.

This persuasive area is in the middle of the brain and is known in neuropsychology as the 'limbic system'. It is subconscious and manages the conscious. It makes decisions, initiates action, conjures up emotion.

If you have an argument by day, you'll probably dream about it by night. A dream is a result of your subconscious Centre Brain processing what has passed through your conscious mind, helping you to work out what it means.

Because your subconscious is in the driving seat, it's important (if you want your communication to persuade and move your audience) that you know how to harness it. Ever tried harnessing a dream – consciously entering it and changing it? It's possible, occasionally. But erratic. Understanding the Centre Brain's five persuasion prompts enables you to begin harnessing the subconscious.

Because the Centre Brain is subconscious, speaking what feels natural to the conscious Outer Brain (where your communication takes off from) won't ready it for the hidden Centre Brain (where it will land). The executives at Pepsi experienced this in Taiwan. The company slogan, 'Come alive with the Pepsi generation', was translated by Taiwanese to mean, 'Pepsi will bring your ancestors back from the dead'.

Learning to speak from the Centre Brain helps you ensure that what you say is readied for an effective landing.

THE TANDEM BRAIN

In many ways, the two brain regions, Outer and Centre Brain, could be compared to two riders on a tandem bike.

Our family owns two tandems: a BMX tandem ridden by our eldest sons and an ancient Claud Butler pedalled by Ruth and me. When we race, the winning team normally gains the edge by managing to ride as one, despite having very different roles. The front rider's role is like the Centre Brain, while the rear rider's role is more like the Outer Brain.

THE CENTRE BRAIN

This is like the front rider. Eyes wide open (yes, you can ride with eyes closed if you're on the back), it uses the images before it to make decisions. What it sees will prompt reaction. It controls the brakes, the gears, the steering. And so it sets direction and makes decisions. The front-rider Centre Brain will ask the rear rider for information on which way to go (the rear rider is less engaged by what it sees, and more motivated by map-reading). The front rider takes its advice into account, though may not always follow it. In an emergency it's the front rider (Centre Brain) that can respond super-fast and use its control to make split-second decisions.

THE OUTER BRAIN

This is like the rear rider – the map-reader. Ascertaining the safest and most direct route, this region advises the front rider, the Centre Brain. It will reach conclusions and communicate them to the front rider. But its contribution is theoretical. It's up to the front rider (Centre Brain) to decide whether to turn it into action. And whether the front rider does, or not, depends on whether what's communicated uses a language that's designed to prompt Centre Brain response.

If today you're trying to persuade someone of something, this picture can help: you're the rear rider on the other person's tandem. He or she is steering. And clear advice or instruction will not prompt the person to steer as you want. Your voice will only stand out when you use the right prompts.

THE POWER OF PROMPTING THE CENTRE BRAIN

My colleagues and I had been asked to help the communications director of a small animal charity. He'd been struggling to win over the members of the board, whom he'd found hard to persuade.

The organization's external communications weren't generating the desired response compared to some of its competitors. When the director of communications had met the board members and made the case for a new direction and approach, his ideas were rejected. There was a persuasion problem internally (the board) and externally (the target audience).

We reframed the communication director's proposal – which the board had rejected – around the Centre Brain's five prompts.

I was invited to sit in on the presentation. I'd been briefed on a long-standing and influential female board member: 'She normally leads the charge after I present,' the comms director explained. 'She'll be sceptical and concerned by what we're proposing. And, if she's very concerned, she'll be the first to stand and will cast doubt on the proposals.'

We'd made sure that each of the Centre Brain's action-prompts was deployed through what was said and also through the presentation on screen. As the communications director finished presenting, what he'd predicted seemed to start happening: the female board member in question rose to her feet. And spoke. I wrote down her words: 'This is the most important thing for the organization in the next five years. This could be worth tens of thousands if we invest in it.'

Other members followed. And I sensed genuine optimism in the room. The board unanimously, even enthusiastically, endorsed the proposals. And, importantly, the endorsement was one of *action*. The board members wanted to know when this proposed change would happen, and what barriers needed to be cleared to enable it. They were expectant.

A MESSAGE ABOUT MANIPULATION

Persuasion is very different from manipulation. One is about pressuring, even tactically bullying, someone into doing what you want (even when it's not the best thing for that individual). The other is about being clear and communicating in a way the person's action brain can grasp.

The five prompts to action laid out in this book don't out-manoeuvre people's ability to evaluate and decide for themselves. If you speak to the Centre Brain, credibility plays a large part. To quote journalist Ed Murrow: 'To be persuasive we must be believable; to be believable we must be credible; to be credible we must be truthful.'[2]

What this book offers comes out of 20 years of development. I attempt to explain – from my limited knowledge of the human brain – which region of the brain the prompts stir. But the prompts are formed on the firm foundation of my experience and effectiveness in TV, radio, magazines, as a main-stage public speaker and as a creative director and brand manager, rather than as a laboratory researcher.

Salman Rushdie said:

> Those who do not have the power of the story that dominates their lives – power to retell it, rethink it, deconstruct it, joke about it and change it as times may change – truly are powerless because they cannot think new thoughts.[3]

Your power in communicating comes from being able to retell, deconstruct and change your communication, while retaining what makes it persuasive. Using a technique without knowing why it works won't stop it working, but it will limit your ability to retell, rethink and change it.

NOT JUST WHAT TO DO, BUT WHY IT WORKS

Wired to Create, by psychologist Scott Barry Kaufman and journalist Carolyn Gregoire, is a brilliantly informative – and deservingly popular – book. It explores the 'ten habits and attributes of highly creative people' in an attempt to 'shed light on the fascinating perplexities of the creative mind'.[4]

These ten habits include: thinking differently, having passion, and daydreaming. *Why* they seem to work isn't explained. That's not the focus of the book. The habits have worked for 'highly creative people' who are worth learning from. But why are they so effective?

Another technique is the popular 'FOAM' model which prescribes use of a Fact, an Opinion, an Anecdote (or story) and a Metaphor to make your communication compelling. I completed the FOAM training but couldn't get to the bottom of why it worked. Why is this model – starting with a 'Fact' – more likely to prompt action than, say, Simon Sinek's excellent model presented in his book *Start with Why*?[5] Or Kaufman's ten habits of highly creative people? Or a currently popular book with the subtitle 'Communication techniques to make you unstoppable'?[6]

Using a technique and not understanding why it works reminds me of a family I met in a very poor part of sub-Saharan Africa. Mum left home at midnight, each night, bucket in hand, walked a staggering four hours to a water source, let her bucket down into the well, and then returned home (another four hours), carrying the container on her head and arriving by morning. Because it was dark by the time she reached the well and let the bucket down, she couldn't see down the hole. But she knew she'd get something.

'Any fool can know', Albert Einstein said. 'The point is to understand.'[7] Without understanding why the technique we use prompts action (or doesn't), we're fumbling around in the dark, like that woman at the well. We're reliant at best on a borrowed light. There's a difference between someone fluent in a language who understands the grammar and can apply the principles, and someone who has memorized key sentences to get them through a specific situation: one can apply his or her knowledge to any situation, while the other always needs the language tutor.

A million communication techniques, all letting their buckets down into the mighty subconscious brain, will all grab *something* (heck, the brains of those you communicate with have the capacity of half the entire world's digital storage – there's plenty of stuff in there!). But will it be something that persuades? Something that prompts the brain to act, rather than just draw conclusions?

This explains the old brainstorming mantra: 'No idea is a bad one.'[8] Without knowing what will prompt response, you have to find out by trial and error. Any insight, idea, statistic or thought *could* be a good one. But once you know what will prompt response, your brainstorming and communication can become much more focused.

The Centre Brain model makes you your own teacher, understanding why any and every technique works or fails. And it equips you to be able to devise your own technique.

The first prompt in persuading people connects to the very heart of how we all read the world around us . . .

THE
BRAIN'S
FIVE
PERSUASION
PROMPTS

'Advertising is fundamentally persuasion, and persuasion happens to be not a science but an art.'
— WILLIAM BERNBACH

'MOST CAMPAIGNS ARE TOO COMPLICATED. THEY REFLECT A LONG LIST OF OBJECTIVES AND TRY TO RECONCILE DIVERGENT VIEWS. UNLESS YOUR CAMPAIGN CONTAINS A BIG IDEA, IT WILL PASS LIKE A SHIP IN THE NIGHT.'

– DAVID OGILVY

3 The message-to-idea metamorphosis principle

Persuasive prompt 1: turn your message into an idea

'Whoever lights a fire controls the match. These prompts put the match in your hand.'

When anyone in our house has a bath, the plants in the garden perk up. It was a simple idea to avoid paying the water company every time we wet the garden. I fitted a £3 plastic junction to the bath wastepipe and, thanks to gravity, all the bathwater now piles down a hose and on to the thirsty plants.

Ideas always contain the answer to a problem, or make sense of an opportunity. As you read about the bathwater, it's likely your brain was picturing something about that idea – and, if you're a fan of gardening, you might have found yourself evaluating it and wondering about its application to your own situation. An English philosopher, Alfred North Whitehead, nailed it when he said, 'Ideas won't keep. Something must be done about them.'[1]

This helps to explain why, as the first prompt-to-action for the Centre Brain, ideas are key.

But ideas are hard to stumble upon. And they often begin in a different form – as a message. This is stage one of the three-part journey from *message* to *idea* to *action*.

You must make your message metamorphose into an idea.

In 'message' form, the above bathwater example reads something like:

> The high reading on the water meter means it's costing loads to keep the garden plants green in the dry patch.

The bath is brought in as part of the *idea* – the answer. The metamorphosis makes the message persuasive by turning it into an idea.

WHAT'S A METAMORPHOSIS?

Imagine a bride arriving for her wedding dressed in jeans and a woolly jumper. True, it's the same bride inside the clothes, but the clothes make all the difference to whether she's going to prompt people to want to photograph her, or inspire her fiancé to believe she's ready to wed, and want to marry her.

A tadpole can't come out of the water, jump or catch worms. But when a metamorphosis happens it can – as a frog. An acorn is at the mercy of a squirrel, until a metamorphosis happens, and it becomes an oak tree that gives the squirrel its food and a place to nest its young. A seed on its own provides negligible food for a hungry person – unless he or she plants it, allowing the metamorphosis to happen so that the seed becomes a crop of food, providing excess seed to store and plant next year.

Messages need to go through a metamorphosis into an idea. If you don't allow the message to find one of its metamorphosed idea-forms, its persuasive power will be minuscule or absent. This needs to happen because messages don't prompt the Centre Brain to action. But as ideas, they do.

This all seems reasonable; surely it's common sense?

ASK A TADPOLE TO JUMP

The difficulty is that our Outer Brains find it easier to deal in messages than ideas. (This is partly because speech is located in the Outer Brain, making it easier to verbalize the messages that are also located there than to host ideas, which are in the Centre Brain.) It's like the toddler who refuses Dad's request to open her mouth and eat the spoonful of food being offered – until it's presented as an idea: 'Here comes a plane! Open up and let it land in your mouth.'

How we package the message changes which part of the brain responds and therefore whether we draw a conclusion ('No, I don't want that dinner') or are prompted to action ('Here comes the plane – I'll open the runway!').

When a tadpole is a tadpole it presumably doesn't feel incomplete (just because it's not yet a frog). So a message might not *feel* inadequate to a task. But ask a tadpole to jump out of the pond and along the bank and it might tell you (if it could speak) that its current form doesn't allow it to do so. In the same way, you might not feel that your message is in any way 'wrong' as a tool for persuading. But its inability to persuade will show you it is, if you attempt to persuade with it.

Ideas are generative: they originate and propagate further thinking, further ideas and the probability of action when they land in our brains.

As Charles F. Brannan brilliantly commented:

> If you have an apple and I have an apple and we exchange these apples then you and I will still each have one apple. But if you have an idea and I have an idea and we exchange these ideas, then each of us will have two ideas.[2]

Ideas generate and release trains of thought. But they go further still: they're absorbed, evolved and changed by the brain they enter – and in turn they change that brain. They stir emotion. Once formed, they are simple and easy to understand, and normally easily visualized.

THE MESSAGE MAGNET

Messages populate our daily conversation. For example:

- 'Does anyone have a phone charger?'
- 'They should not have signed that striker!'
- 'I've got an invite to their party!'
- 'Did you have a good holiday?'
- 'What time shall I come over?'
- 'It's going to snow tomorrow!'
- 'I've decided to resign!'
- 'Could you drop me in town?'
- 'Did you hear about that earthquake?'

These are all messages. And when we try to persuade someone of something, it's normally messages – facts, details and opinions – that we deploy to try to convince. They do awaken a *part* of the brain, but it's the wrong part. They speak to and awaken the Outer Brain, which receives the information, analyses, and reaches a conclusion (which is very different from deciding to act or respond).

Try today observing whether effective, and ineffective, communicators are using an idea or a message as their persuasion tool – and how effective it is.

In the 1940s a linguist named Benjamin Lee Whorf claimed that speakers of the Native American language Hopi and speakers of English saw the world differently because of the differences in their languages. He suggested that because the English language deals with time as chunks (hours, minutes, days), English speakers see time as a thing to invest, use or lose. The Hopi language, Whorf said, doesn't deal with time in this way, instead framing it as one continuous cycle, which alters how Hopi speakers see the world.[3]

Having a discussion that is based on ideas will leave you with a different feeling from that caused by a factual conversation led by a message. You'll see the world differently because you're using a different part of the brain, which speaks a different language.

The idea that a particular language brings with it a different perspective on the world is true in our bilingual brains.

Speech and words live, in your brain and mine, in the same area as rational facts, details, opinions and information ('what' and 'how' information).You can answer What and How questions ('What's your name?' 'How did you get here?') very quickly because that information is held in word form.

Ideas live in a different part of the brain. When you begin to discuss ideas (especially new and evolving ones), you may find it takes a little bit longer to verbalize them.This is because that part of the brain has a different language: pictures. So your brain has to 'export' them from the subconscious Centre Brain to the mouth via your Outer Brain.

What does all this mean for how persuasive you are – and can become? It means you'll most naturally veer towards speaking a language which doesn't activate the action-and-response centre of the brain. Learning the language that this Centre Brain area understands is therefore important if you want to activate it when you communicate.

POLITICIANS

Politicians provide us with a great case study.When under pressure, their brains apparently revert to facts, details and opinions, as revealed by Gordon Brown when he was Prime Minister and facing a tense press briefing in April 2009. The late parliamentary sketch-writer Simon Hoggart captured it brilliantly:

> Two British TV reporters asked, in effect, the same question: what's in all this for your voters? What they wanted was a soundbite for the news, something like, 'safer homes, safer jobs, and a quicker end to the crisis', perhaps. Now Gordon Brown does not do soundbites. Instead he does bread and

butter puddings, great bowls full of stodge, lumpy with facts, judgements and declarations. You could almost sense the despair back at TV centre as his reply went on and on.[4]

But this is not true of all politicians. It's interesting to note how much Winston Churchill did the opposite, turning all his messages into ideas. We can also see the impact these had in drawing engagement and action from people as they approached the situation before them. In his 1940 'Blood, Toil, Tears and Sweat' speech he introduced the idea of victory (and used the *picture* of a long road) rather than concentrating on facts-and-detail information: 'You ask what is our aim? . . . Victory. Victory at all costs. Victory in spite of all terror. Victory, however long and hard the road may be.'[5]

One of the best examples of the power of an idea to stir action is Churchill's famous 'Never Surrender' speech to the UK House of Commons; his words gained traction and helped establish the policy of 'no surrender'. Analysis suggests it 'made people feel they were not alone in the struggle against Hitler'.[6]

We shall defend our island whatever the cost. We shall fight on the beaches, we shall fight on the landing grounds, we shall fight in the fields and in the streets. We shall fight in the hills. We shall never surrender.[7]

Many see Churchill as one of the greatest orators of the twentieth century. Fewer people talk about the fact that he practised his speeches for hours and hours: he was not in fact a natural public orator and carried a slight stammer and lisp. However, his intentionality in forming his speeches allowed his messages to metamorphose into ideas, so that they landed in the Centre Brain, giving them power to change his listeners' perspectives.

Churchill understood that how he structured and framed what he said gave his speeches the power to (literally) change the course of history. He was not a believer in throwing a speech out into the dark, hoping it might ignite something.

#SHREDDED

Advertisers rarely communicate their message directly – in message form. They first find an idea, because they know that will stick. Sit and watch an ad-break on TV and ask yourself, for each advert, what the message is, and then what idea the creators have employed to make the message sticky. You'll see just how different, even unrelated, the two are.

At first glance Shredded Wheat might not grab you. It's a healthy cereal (if a little bland) and useful if you need fibre. But the product itself isn't enough to make you buy it. That's why a recent Shredded Wheat TV ad mentions the actual cereal only once and never names the message, which is 'Buy Shredded Wheat'. Instead, it kicks off with a slo-mo shot of a 30-something man diving off a high board into an outdoor swimming pool, with this voice-over underneath:

> Boom! There he is. The man who made the decision to take life to the high board. To bravely throw himself into that great chlorinated unknown . . . and in the eyes of his young son, this daddy of all daddies, filled with

100% wholegrain Shredded Wheat, is shredding life.
Shredding that hotel high board.
#shredded

NO ONE BUYS THE PRODUCT

While the *message* behind the Shredded Wheat ad is still about a healthy cereal, the *idea* in the 'Hotel High Board' advert has nothing obvious to do with the cereal. That's the mark of a strong idea – not that it directly reflects the product (or your message about it) but that it introduces a memorable lens through which people can see the product (or message about it).

And this attracts the attention of the Centre Brain.

In this case, 'Shredding life – Shredded Wheat' wraps the cereal in the idea that you can experience life head-on, impressing those you're close to, just by eating the stuff. It's the idea, not the message, which people buy, which awakens the Centre Brain, which prompts response.

Branding and marketing is about wrapping. Communication is about wrapping. The wrapping is what people buy. And the wrapping is the idea that has the power to earn a place in the brain's action centre. Businessman and author Peter Nivio Zarlenga said, 'In our factory we make lipstick. In our advertising we sell hope.'[8] Just as people don't buy the product but buy the idea the product is wrapped in, people you try to persuade will not buy your message unless it's wrapped in an idea. The idea makes them feel good, and act.

When you next struggle to gain traction with something you're trying to persuade someone to do, ask yourself whether you've made the message metamorphose into an idea. That's what will gain the traction. Without that, as a message, it will prompt the brain's firewall defence, which will sideline your message.

In 2009, research at the University of Athens found that readers' responses to headlines in UK and US newspapers favoured 'uninformative and creative' headlines. Looking at the actual headlines, it's clear that those with an 'idea' strongly beat those based on a 'message'. People read headlines that 'rivet[ed] their attention' – for example, 'The smell of corruption, the scent of truth' – over ones which simply laid out the message, or tried to 'sell the product'.[9]

In theatre terms, it's like a no-props monologue (one performer, one stool, nothing else) versus a full stage of actors in a full set. The narrative may be just as exciting in the monologue as in the full performance. But the single actor has to deliver it all. The idea is like the set on a stage which, literally, sets the stage for the idea to be performed. It's an activator to awaken the Centre Brain. Without it, you're starting from ground zero – you're a monologue performer.

YOUR TEMPLATE FIREWALL

If your doorbell sounds in the next five minutes and a salesperson is offering to redo your windows, your Outer Brain will deploy one of its 'templates'. We all have templates, stored ready to deflect things our Centre Brains do not want to act on. Your stored template for a door salesperson might be 'I'm just about to eat' or 'We're not interested in having new windows'. Or, if a charity chugger accosts you in town, 'I already give to charity' may be the template. You'll have templates for responding to 'How are you?' Templates to describe your job, your family, your hobbies. Everything.

Our brains are powerful in their ability to close down unwanted intrusions or interruptions, and to negotiate, filter and prioritize regular engagements: they use a 'template firewall' to do this.

Remember the last time your persuasiveness missed its mark? It drew a general nod of agreement, but without action or intentional response? That's you hitting someone's template firewall.

The good news? There *is* a way past it. Ideas. They are your route to navigate past your audience's Outer Brain templates to the Centre Brain's action button.

Ideas are novel. That's why the Centre Brain loves them. And you can't predict the hidden power of persuasion available once an idea awakens the Centre Brain.

I was visiting Suzanna, a good friend, at university on the weekend her halls of residence were holding (unofficial) floor parties. The students on each floor covered those on another floor on their party night, using a simple early-warning system to alert them to any campus staff members who came to investigate the noise. The campus Student Code meant this sort of late-night event would bring trouble if those involved were caught.

My friend's party was in full swing when a breathless second-floor student charged in: trouble was on its way. By the time the hall master arrived, the music had been killed and over a hundred students had vanished.

In Suzanna's room about 30 students stood in darkness. The knock came, and Suzanna, in pyjamas and dressing gown, hair looking slept on, opened the door. Muttering something about how late it was, she asked, 'Why did you wake me?'

The hall master asked how she had not heard the music, apologized and knocked on the next door – to the same staged response.

What you see when you awaken a template (the Outer Brain) is what the hall master saw: someone wanting to get rid of your intrusion. A different signal awakens a different response. Ten minutes after the hall master had gone, a different signal came which awakened a very different response: the lights and music (slightly quieter) went on and the room was suddenly full of life and energy. Same room, very different engagement.

The Centre Brain of everyone you communicate with has a 'novelty centre' (the *substantia nigra* or ventral segmental area). Speaking to it with an idea is like giving a 'let the party begin' signal: action will follow.

IDEAS AND INCUBATORS

The power of an idea is substantial. For good, and bad.

Joseph Stalin, who became a state dictator in the Soviet Union in 1924, said, 'Ideas are more powerful than guns. We would not let our enemies have guns; why should we let them have ideas?'[10] In Germany, on 1 September 1932, Joseph Goebbels, who would the following year become Nazi Germany's Minister of Propaganda, published an article entitled 'Advice for a Dictator and for Those Who Want to Become One'. In it he wrote, 'If the idea is lacking, it is impossible.'[11]

I recall the day our chickens laid their first egg. Two of my sons, Aidan and Oscar, had been running down to the chicken house, morning after morning, in hope of an egg. We'd watched the chickens hatch in an incubator in our kitchen, and hand-reared them. Looking back, it's clear to me that the 'idea' that a live bird could emerge from an egg, so long as the children turned the eggs daily and kept the heat and humidity constant, sparked more ideas in the two boys. We sourced pallets, stripped them and built a huge chicken coop complete with nesting box. And when the birds started laying, we bought a book detailing countless recipes one could make with eggs.

The eggs enabled my sons to see possibilities and engage in them. As French poet and author Antoine de Saint-Exupéry put it: 'A pile of rocks ceases to be a rock when somebody contemplates it with the idea of a cathedral in mind.'[12]

British entrepreneur Sir Richard Branson was asked to write a letter to a younger version of himself. In 'My Letter to 10-Year-Old Me' he wrote, 'Your imagination is one of your greatest gifts. Your ability to think differently will become one of your biggest advantages in life – taking you places where most straight-A students will never go.'[13]

I overheard a graphic designer I work with discussing with another designer something he had found useful when he hit a brick wall on coming up with an idea. 'When I'm struggling to think of an idea or concept, sometimes I'll go to sleep frustrated but then wake up with the exact idea I need in my head and will get to work on it,' he explained. When I asked him, he was able to give a powerful recent example in which his subconscious Centre Brain had clearly processed the creative challenge while he slept and offered him the solution in a dream. Since Leonardo da Vinci first asked the question over 500 years ago, I'm not sure we've made huge progress in answering it: 'Why does the eye see a thing more clearly in dreams than the imagination when awake?'[14]

Ideas do grow through imagination. But their starting block is normally a simple fact, detail or opinion. Or, put another way, a message. When our communication fails to progress beyond information, and we don't change it into idea form, we should not be surprised that response is slow.

But this is our choice. We can spark ideas if we decide to!

YOU HOLD THE MATCH

One bonfire night we invited friends over, lit a large fire and set off fireworks. Eagerly, I set off a super-sized rocket, so tall that it needed to be bedded tightly into a bucket of sand to prevent toppling. Too tightly as it turned out. The rocket couldn't lift off and detonated at ground level. People dived for cover. (Thankfully no one was injured.)

One of our friends with infant children had been watching from an upstairs bedroom. Above the din of everyone recounting what had just happened, we didn't hear her frantically banging on the window. From her vantage point she could see several of the large rocket-sparks land in our wood store, igniting the plastic cover and then setting the wood alight.

Fortunately, someone eventually heard her banging – and the hose did the trick! But the lesson? When you take a match in your hand you unleash huge power. You may not understand the chemical process happening as the paper and kindling catch and start throwing out heat, but you don't need to. You just need a match.

In a similar way, turning your message into an idea alongside the other brain-prompts puts the match in your hand. They make your persuasion effective. *Not* using the correct assets – as I failed to do when I launched the rocket – means the outcome becomes sporadic and hard to predict. Chapter 10 offers some specific and practical ways to begin to make a message metamorphose into an idea.

'THERE ARE TWO GREAT
DAYS IN A PERSON'S LIFE –
THE DAY WE ARE BORN AND
THE DAY WE DISCOVER WHY.'
– WILLIAM BARCLAY

4 The Why-first principle

Persuasive prompt 2: 'why' makes 'what' and
'how' interesting

'People are people . . .   Think of one thing you're going
their brains function the   to do this week. Anything. And
same, respond to the same   ask yourself *why* you're going to
prompts.'   do it. There's the route to the heart
of your motivations. What matters
is why. Always. And in everything. We can see the 'what' – but
normally have to unearth the 'why' behind it. 'Why' is the second
of the Centre Brain's prompts to action.

In the 1970s a man in Surrey went into his garden and started
digging a hole. *What* he was doing was obvious (and fairly boring
to passers-by). *How* he was doing it was self-explanatory (with a
spade). But as people understood *why* he was digging, they began
to stop and take note. The previously boring What and How were
suddenly made interesting. The man – a friend of my father – was
responding to a drought in the UK, and subsequent water short-
age. Having a young family and a thirsty garden, and faced with

limited water, he decided to dig until he found water in his garden. He got deep.

Why is always the connector because it lets you decide quickly if you relate to what's going on. In *The Lovemarks Effect*, Kevin Roberts writes, 'People will only respond when you touch their own personalities, dreams and desires. When you understand what attracts them.'[1] The Why behind what you say or do is what bridges this gap. People recognize in *your* Why something which attracts *them*. It speaks to their own personalities. It's the link.

Despite the fact that talking about What and How, without the Why, makes you a much less persuasive version of yourself, you'll still instinctively veer to the What and How ahead of Why.

But why is this?

WHERE CONNECTION GROWS

Because of where speech is located, it's easier to ask and answer What and How questions over Why questions. When did you last get introduced to someone and instead of 'What's your name?' start with 'Why did your parents choose that name?' Or instead of 'Do you live locally?' start with 'Why do you live where you live?' Social norms rightly protect us from doing that. Asking for facts creates a safe early-conversation zone. But if you watch a single friend who is clearly attracted to another single friend you've introduced him to, you'll notice he'll instinctively progress much faster from the What and How to the Why. He'll be craving connection, which is found in answer to Why questions.

If you're single and you struggle to connect well when you meet someone you like, spend time in advance working out how to pull off a seamless transition from What to Why. If you're writing a profile on an online dating site, any What and How needs to be wrapped in Why, to be read *through* Why.

Ruth and I once applied to Channel 4's home-move show, *Location, Location, Location*, with Phil Spencer and Kirstie Allsopp. The show was popular and the website was clear that applications might never be answered as the production team was dealing with an overwhelming number. I therefore answered all the What and How questions with a Why lens through which I made sense of the What and How, and employed all the Centre Brain prompts. I wrote only half of my online application, before saving it to finish it the following evening. The next day the show's producers called me. I warned them I had not completed the application, but they were clear: they liked what they read and would like to proceed with our application – as soon as we had a buyer. (To enable participants to offer a purchase price for any homes Phil and Kirstie showed them, they had to have an offer in place on the house they were selling.) We had our home on the market for four months but couldn't find a buyer, so we never got on to the show to find the unusual project-property we'd dreamt of. But the point's clear: Why prompts action and response in situations where What or How struggle to.

Everything needed in a conversation with deeper connection and persuasion potential sits in the Centre Brain. As Chapter 7 outlines, that's where emotion lives. And because speech doesn't live there, the Why questions and answers need translation, into word form, from the way they're subconsciously stored – as pictures and ideas. That's why it's easier to ask and answer 'What's your name?' than 'Why are you excited about this week [or month or year]?' The Outer Brain is a little like a conveyor belt at the supermarket. Stuff that happens each day is like the shopping that's loaded on, checked through, bagged up and taken away at the other end. Very little on the conveyor belt makes a lasting impression. When it does, the Centre Brain steps in and diverts it on to a conveyor belt that goes to the kitchen where the food is prepared, eaten and turned into energy – or action.

This explains why prompting a response to your communication requires you to serve up a different first course: the Why.

Your key memory structures are in the middle of your brain, in a part called the hippocampus. Research shows that the Outer Brain is weaker at retaining memories.[2]

ADVERTISERS ASK WHY

A quick scan of campaigns that seek to persuade you to respond, in the charity and corporate sectors, reveals that advertisers rarely start with what their organization does, or what their product is, or how they do it. They start with why they do it. This is the language that awakens the Centre Brain and can prompt it to action and response.

Save the Children's What reads:

> We run world-class programmes to save children's lives . . .

This was translated into Why form in a recent (and very successful) campaign, titled 'No Child Born to Die'.

Adidas makes sports kits – that's the company's What. But its strapline takes the Why road, answering why you need Adidas products if you want to achieve in sport:

> Impossible is nothing.

Specsavers sells glasses, not through showing us what *type* of glasses we might want, but through explaining why we need them. The company had a hugely successful campaign using the slogan:

> Should've gone to Specsavers.

In this campaign, each ad answers the Why (the reason you should have gone to a Specsavers shop):

- A middle-aged man mistakenly stumbles into a steamy sauna, naked. As the steam clears, he realizes that he's in a chef's kitchen.
- A vet, frantically searching for the pulse on a cat he's treating, shouts to his assistant, 'Got a cat with no pulse, need an IV line!' The assistant quickly grabs the 'cat' – revealing it to be a fluffy hat.
- A policeman conducting a door-to-door search for a criminal holds up an exact photo-match of the man at the door, then says, 'Be sure to keep an eye out, sir.'

A 'Giving Tuesday' email from Charity: Water invites recipients to

> Give opportunity . . . Give help . . . hope . . . education
> . . . time . . .

These options flash through the email, each one speaking about why giving water (water being the What) is so important:

> Invest in a world where everyone has clean water by giving monthly.

Apple's What is technology – computers, laptops, phones. The company markets and sells these as a Why, a way of thinking, an approach to life:

> Think different.

Vauxhall made the Why absolutely blatant in a recent set of Corsa commercials. The ad, featuring an attractive female driver who is reverse-parking effortlessly, asks:

> Can a car make you look amazing?

'Advanced park-assist' technology is the What that the company is offering, but this is seen through the lens of the Why that it enables: so that you look amazing.

At face value, NatWest Bank's slogan might imply just a bunch of friendly bank clerks making a mundane lunchtime visit to the bank a little easier:

> Helpful banking.

That phrase would answer what the bank does and how it does it. And would have gone on to the Outer Brain's conveyor belt, and off. Instead, in a recent TV ad campaign NatWest elevates the Why, using emotive footage of the contrast between good and bad in the world, and then positioning the bank slap bang in the middle of all the moving footage of what's good in the world.

Why bank with us, ask the people at NatWest? Because, according to this ad,

> We are doing the right thing.

They do this not just for you, but for society and the world. The slogan provides an interpretation of their What: 'Helpful banking'.

MIRROR, MIRROR, IN THE BRAIN

Imagine spotting a local teenager preventing one of her peers from crossing a street. You wonder what on earth she's doing and why, but you walk on, feeling little desire to get involved – little connection.

Your brain contains something called 'mirror neurons'. If you spend several hours in a coffee shop with a good friend, your brain's mirror neurons will align your breathing with his; in other words, our brains are built to *connect*. And the degree to which you understand *why* is the degree to which you'll experience the emotional connection.

When you do understand why, you get the whole picture and your Centre Brain has the key to engage and prompt action. Back to that street where the teen is stopping her peer crossing the road. As you walk on, you understand – as the young person did – the Why: an angry-looking dog is crouching behind a wall, apparently ready to jump. The teenager is, in fact, protecting her friend. Knowing the Why immediately creates connection. And makes you consider getting involved. That's your mirror neurons generating emotion in your Centre Brain, mirroring what you're seeing.

The mirror neurons rely on Why. When you communicate without explaining the Why, people will walk on by.

Mirror neurons are yours to activate by communicating the Why. My three-word guide when approaching a friend, colleague or group – to convince someone of something – is this:

People are people.

Outwardly people may differ – you may speak to a corporate 'suit' with a severe face, or to an attractive peer with some nice body-art down the arm. But their brains function the same, respond to the same prompts. So stick to the prompts. Especially when you feel (as you are likely to) a tendency in yourself to divert the conversation away from Why to What and How – to those reliable (if a little boring) facts. Your dependence on and preference for communicating What and How – facts – will increase in direct relation to your feelings of inferiority in front of an audience. This in turn decreases your chances of persuading that audience to accept your point of view. The point is: a person's life experience doesn't freeze the brain against the prompts outlined in this book.

Several years ago, I travelled with Marcus, a very experienced photographer who had flown to 52 different countries the previous year photographing cases of human suffering. A girl we met, and her story, brought even him to tears. Experience had not dulled his Centre Brain's sensitivity.

You may wonder whether seasoned and experienced people are less likely to be moved to action when you prompt their Centre Brain. The answer is that the Centre Brain remains open to prompts whether you're 19 or 90. And whether you're a master of your area, or a novice.

SPEAK FIRST - THEN SATISFY

One of my favourite mottos is:

> Speak to the Centre Brain (using Why), then satisfy the Outer Brain (using What and How).

In that order. That means, try to awaken the Centre Brain by using the language it responds to: Why. Then introduce the details – the What and How – through the Why lens you've put in place.

What does this look like?

Think about what you did today. Those What and How facts are not likely to be engaging. Think now of why you did what you did. That's how What finds its punch.

I went to watch my sons play football in local leagues this morning. That's the What. And that's unengaging for you. Even boring. But if I start with *why* I went, it brings the What to life.

I never played football as a boy. Always chosen last to play in the school football teams, and at church the monthly youth-group 'footy night' saw me try – and fail – to acquire some skills. When I was eight years old we moved 200 miles from home because of my dad's job; several years later I returned for a long-awaited reunion with my old friends, and I panicked to hear they'd planned a day of football. It was hell.

It was when I read Malcolm Gladwell's book *Outliers* that I finally understood: 10,000 hours doing anything makes you pretty damn good at it. World-class, in fact. But *not* doing 'deliberate practice' means you won't perform when it matters.[3] I'd never practised football!

With three sons I always knew the day would come. And it did when, aged four, my second son, Oscar, asked to play football. So we did. His energy for it attracted my eldest son Aidan, then aged six, to join in. We played every Saturday and Sunday in the garden, all year round. Year on year. As we practised, we *all* learned. The grass died, and a permanent bare-earth pitch was born. I pulled some old scaffold poles out of a skip and erected goalposts. We got a floodlight for winter evenings, and my youngest son Eben was soon joining in.

Our weekends are now full of football. My eldest son captains the school football team and was recently 'signed' to a team in the Champions' League of the Surrey Youth League. My middle son plays in Saturday, and Sunday, leagues and for the school team, and my youngest son has been picked for a local league.

Watching football is, therefore, for me, about believing that what you are able to do is a reflection of what you've deployed of your potential *so far*. That's the Why. If you are either not persuasive at all, or sometimes persuasive or rarely persuasive, it's because you've yet to deploy your potential and begin practising the prompts in this book.

Identifying the Why, and starting with it, is where this begins.

THE SIX-WORD STORY

Many years ago, famous story-writer Ernest Hemingway made a bet, during a meal out with friends, that he could write a story in six words. He did. He scribbled the story on a napkin, passed it round – and won the money. What made his story work was the Why.

> For sale. Baby shoes. Never worn.

On reading it, we find the What boring (shoes for sale). But the Why (why are they for sale – what happened to the baby?) engages us.

Everything has a Why to it. If you do one thing today, intentionally look out for those Whys. The more familiar you become with Why, the more you understand its power. So when your boss gives you the data (the What), ask for the analysis and application (the Why). When your best friend says she *needs* to go shopping, ask why. What's the story? It may be boredom – or something deeper. When you feel stirred by or connected to someone on

TV, or at work or a party, you'll know your Centre Brain is responding to a Why. Look for it. Why? Because you'll begin to notice how much more engaging it is talking with people who offer the Why and not just the What. And when *you* communicate with the Why, it will make what you say persuasive.

Hemingway's six-word story uses a popular vehicle for communicating Why: the story. In the past two years, 'story' has led the way for a growing number of communication companies.

I received a marketing email recently which captures the growing belief that stories are the answer:

> Storytelling is the foundation of every great content-marketing strategy. It is not only confined to B2C brands as more and more B2B brands start taking bigger risks by reaching out to prospects in new and interesting ways. Take for example this year's winners at Cannes Lions who are telling great stories across a whole host of digital platforms!

But why do stories work? And how do they connect to the Centre Brain prompts?

ARE YOU DOCTOR OR PATIENT?

You know stories work. They're (rightly) the bedrock for a huge amount of persuasive communication. But have you wrestled with *why* they're so effective (if for no other reason than allowing you to evaluate whether story is the tool you need for a particular situation)?

Stories work – they engage people, persuade people and prompt response – because they create pictures and answer the Why: they activate several of the Centre Brain's prompts. This means that any other communication tool that creates a picture, and answers the Why, can have the same persuasive potential. For example, a friend of mine, who paints, prompts emotion and response through his paintings. When I returned from West Africa recently, I brought with me a basket made by the members of the family which hosted me. Whenever food ran out, they went to the river, harvested wild reeds and made breadbaskets. Each basket took five days to weave and was a beautiful product, and when sold at market it paid for two meals' worth of food. The physical item represented the need. I purchased one from them and brought it back, using it as 'the story' when speaking at various events: the members of one family in famine, without any bread, make breadbaskets to sell, but by making them they become more and more hungry – their baskets more and more empty.

The Centre Brain prompts unlock your persuasiveness because they let you understand what buttons you need to press, releasing you to find many ways to press them. When you're using a system or prescribed technique, you have only that way to communicate. Many of these systems are brilliant and very effective. Centre Brain is not in competition with them. Rather, it helps *explain* them, and enables you, when you use them, to explore and expand them because you understand which prompt they're activating.

A CASE STUDY: LONDON 2012

It was Why that won, for the city of London, a race no one expected it to win – the race to host the 2012 Olympic Games.

The press reported that a win for Paris was a foregone conclusion. On the day of the announcement of the winning bid, all but three of the 57 photographers present at the venue were waiting in front of the Paris delegation; this fact alone testifies that something unexpected had happened. That no one expected London to win.

What occurred was, according to a man I know who was present, a last-minute switch of votes – just enough to remove Paris's convincing lead and give the race to London. And it came down to London being the only city whose representatives, at the crucial final moment, spoke to the Centre Brain with Why, rather than to the Outer Brain with What.

A rule change meant that no member of the Olympic Committee could visit cities whose bids had reached the final. Instead, in the final rounds, each city's team was invited to show a short film to sell its city. The Paris representatives pulled out all the stops, bringing in Luc Besson (director of *Taken 2*) to make their film. New York's offering was directed by Steven Spielberg. Together with Moscow and Madrid, all the teams made films which focused on what they could offer – the facts. The problem was that the information that made their cities outstanding host options for the 2012 Olympics (transport infrastructure; warmth of locals; world-famous landmarks) filled their films but didn't touch the Centre Brains of the judges on the viewing panel, or prove persuasive. The Paris, Moscow and New York teams set their films within their cities. The London team didn't.

The representatives for London knew they'd nothing to lose. This released them to break with expectation and speak to the Why.

Apart from two references to 'London 2012', the city did not feature in script or visuals in London's film. Instead of showing what London had in terms of services and infrastructure, or how London could make the 2012 games a success, the film-makers focused on young people from around the world, rich and poor. The film began in Africa, making the case for why London should host: because London could reconnect the Olympic ideals to millions of young people and use the 2012 games to inspire youths all over the world to choose sport.

The film drew heavily on all the Centre Brain prompts: creating a powerful *idea* (that sport could lift young people's horizons to help them fulfil their potential), *pictorializing* that idea (showing young people from poor backgrounds rising to a global stage) and answering *why* in the final message of the film:

> London will inspire the champions of tomorrow.

What happened caught 54 of the 57 photographers by surprise. Fights broke out in their scramble to move from the delegation of the expected winners – Paris – to that of London. Those who made the film knew it carried risk. But they were in the (fortunate) position of knowing they had little to lose. And they discovered just how powerful it can be to answer the Why first, as the route to convincing the brain to act. Decisively.

You can watch the films on Vimeo: enter 'London 2012 bid' and watch that city's production. Then watch the Paris, New York and Moscow bid films for a stark contrast of What and How approaches.

NOT A COINCIDENCE

Communicating for action is like farming: what you reap will be the result of what you sowed – or, often, what you said. It's not a coincidence. When you use the prompts, including Why, the brain can be persuaded to act, or not. It's the communication version of GIGO: 'Garbage In, Garbage Out'. Or vice versa.

What does this mean for you? If you embed the prompts-to-action covered in this book in your communications until the prompts are normal for you, you shrink the 'chance' factor in your efforts to persuade.

This is a journey worth embarking on – one that can influence the direction of your life.

More than 100 years ago my Welsh great-grandfather, Ben, looked down some railway tracks and changed path. He'd had an argument with his father. He packed, left home, headed to the station and got on the first train. The train's destination was Fishguard, Wales. Arriving in the town, and knowing no one, he asked the station master where he might find lodgings. The man gave him directions to the home of a family with a guest room available.

Ben took lodgings there and was (I imagine, though I have no proof!) very pleased to meet Hannah, the daughter of the family. They fell in love, married, and had five children, one of them my grandmother. They spent the rest of their lives happily married in Fishguard (where they're now resting in peace).

The first step of any journey can be scary, and what follows will not happen without that frightening first step. But the rewards make this journey worthwhile. For you, today.

When I was interviewed for a job in TV, I had (I later found out) the least experience of all the applicants. It was a job that normally drew upwards of 2,000 applications. I was shortlisted and knew I had to speak to the action centre of the interviewers' brains. So when I was asked any question (and most were What and How questions), I answered with Why answers to establish a context, and through that came on to the What and How. This created connection. And I got the job.

'WHAT GOOD IS THE WARMTH OF SUMMER WITHOUT THE COLD OF WINTER TO GIVE IT SWEETNESS?'

– JOHN STEINBECK

The contrasting-options principle

Persuasive prompt 3: contrast in communication, speeds response

'You can speed the rate of decision by prompting the Centre Brain to evaluate two options against each other.'

Contrast is a compass for your Centre Brain, helping it to decide which course to take. It does this by providing the Centre Brain's 'weighing scales' with options for each end of the scales to weigh against each other. Your Centre Brain uses contrast in many ways: each of your eyes receives a slightly different picture of what you look at, and your brain uses the contrast to help determine distance. So too the Centre Brain looks for contrast in the pictures, opportunities, information and ideas it receives, to help it make decisions.

By 'polarizing' options, you help to prompt action.

In TV production there's a saying:

Make them mad, sad or glad – but not apathetic.

This slogan captures how news programmes and features work. Their impact happens through contrast – always showing the opposite side of a story. When I was working in live TV early in my career, my colleagues and I responded to a story about an MP who had publicly said that young people should sleep with their girlfriends or boyfriends before considering deeper commitment, to help them explore compatibility. The managing editor instinctively looked for the contrast to that scenario, namely, waiting to have sex until you marry. I was asked, as an engaged 22-year-old who had decided with Ruth to wait to have sex until we were married, to sit opposite the MP on live TV and offer a contrasting opinion.

Why is contrast so important? Because it prompts action. When people feel strongly about something, they react – they take action. And contrast enables that. The studio phones rang and rang with calls from the public after that feature on sex before marriage. Contrast works like the pendulum in a clock: to go one way, the pendulum has to first go the other. Each side provides momentum for the other side.

Contrast is the Centre Brain's third prompt to action. Once you've got the attention of that part of the brain using ideas and the Why, you can speed the *rate of decision* by prompting the Centre Brain to evaluate two options against each other.

CONTRAST TURNS AN OK OFFER INTO A GREAT OFFER

I was knocked off my motorbike several years back. The garage told me I was looking at a repair bill of £500. This was very bad news – an unexpected expense. In the event, the bill was nearer £200. And I felt hugely relieved, even elated. My brain was contrasting the two potential costs. Although £200 was still an unexpected cost, my brain evaluated it next to the alternative of £500 and left me somehow feeling *pleased* about it. The brain uses contrast to determine reactions and response. But if in your communication you fail to provide contrast, the Centre Brain will itself provide something to contrast with the one thing you've given it. And this 'contrast' is normally a 'do nothing' option.

The more you recognize contrast as vital to persuasion, the more you spot it being used. I was recently approached about a campaign I'm involved in, based in the USA. The offer, from an advertising agent, was to run a series of adverts in a prime spot, on a huge screen, in a popular public area in one of the USA's biggest cities. Without contrast, the offer was simply to buy three months of advertising at $30,000. But the offer, and price, had been wrapped in contrast, making it seem significantly more attractive. This is how the advertiser used contrast to make the offer more persuasive. The agent told me:

- These advertising opportunities always sold well in advance – demand was high. This was an unusual last-minute opportunity, allowing the offer of an advantageous price.
- A client had the three-month slot booked, but had to pull out at the last minute, allowing our campaign to step to the front of the queue for a normally competitive advertising opportunity.
- The client who had booked the slot, and pulled out, had paid the majority of the normal $140,000 price for the three months.

This meant we'd only have to pay the final amount of $30,000 for advertising worth four times that amount.

SCALES IN THE BRAIN

Imagine you're trying to convince someone that she should buy a car you're selling. Picture a set of scales in her brain. For a decision to be made, something must be on each end of the scales: the brain will weigh both ends against each other to make a decision. If you give the prospective buyer only one option, her brain will need to fill the other end of the scales. And it's likely to put there the option of *not* buying the car.

If, instead, you give the Centre Brain two choices, you fill both ends of the scale, and the Centre Brain focus will remain on those two rather than needing to introduce its own 'don't buy' option.

For example: you can buy the car either for £1,000 without the extra speakers, or £1,100 *with* the speakers (worth £300) included. The brain will not focus on 'Don't buy the car' (unless it sees good reasons not to buy the car). Instead it will weigh up the two options you've offered against each other – both being to buy the car.

If you go to a garage to look at cars, and the showroom has only one model of the car you want, your brain will take longer to form an opinion, and will place 'Look around for another option' on the other end of the scales to contrast with the car in front of you. If you're shown two comparable cars, your Centre Brain will find it easier to reach a decision quickly.

This is vital for persuasive communication. When you communicate, providing the Centre Brain with two options for response or action will mean it's more likely that one of those responses will be chosen. This is something advertisers know and use, as the following examples demonstrate.

A HUNDRED YEARS OF HATE – MARMITE

The makers of the yeast-based extract Marmite have built their brand on polarizing opinion with their slogan:

> Love it or hate it.

So successful has the idea been that it's entered the English language as a way to refer to anything that splits opinion: 'That's marmite.' By giving the Centre Brain contrast, the producers of Marmite prompt consumers to decide: which side am I on? And a decision is better than apathy – it's the first step towards buying the product. The 'Love It or Hate It' campaign was launched in 1996 after five years of slow sales. In the following five years the popularity of the brand grew by five per cent *each year* to where it now sits with sales valued at £25 million a year.

FOSTERS

The biggest response to any beer ad (according to the Institute of Practitioners in Advertising (IPA)) was prompted by a series of TV commercials titled 'Good Call!' These featured two Aussie guys, in a beach shack, surrounded by attractive young women and taking phone calls from worried British men. The contrast was between Brad and Dan, who (with beer can in hand) represented Fosters, and nervous-looking men, who called up worried and became confident.

The ads helped Fosters to regain market leadership and won the IPA Effectiveness Awards Grand Prix in 2014.

JOHN LEWIS

Another award-winning series of ads is the John Lewis Christmas series, in which each advert is built around contrast of some kind. The 2011 ads, titled 'The Long Wait', featured a little boy waiting for Christmas, to a soundtrack of the song 'Let Me Get What I Want', and generated additional sales estimated at more than £1 billion. Warm and humorous, the storyline features a contrast between the rest of the year, which is waiting time, and the arrival of Christmas. On Christmas morning the boy leaps out of bed to find a stocking overflowing with presents. A second layer of contrast then appears, between giving and receiving, when he runs past the presents to his wardrobe, grabs a gift he's been storing there, and runs to his parents' room as the message appears:

> For gifts you can't wait to give.

Every John Lewis Christmas ad has been built around contrast. In a 2007 advert, adult presents were opened by children, contrasting the past and present with the line:

> Remember how Christmas used to feel? Give someone that feeling.

In 'The Bear and the Hare' (2013) the idea hangs on the contrast between a bear who appears disengaged from Christmas and his friend, a hare, who nevertheless leaves a gift in his cave. The bear appears, smiling, on Christmas morning – the gift turning out to be a clock, an antidote to bears' normal lie-ins. 'Monty the Penguin' (2014) was hung on the contrast between togetherness and isolation: everyone has someone – a friend or partner – but Monty has no one.

In 2015, the John Lewis 'Man on the Moon' ad contrasted youth (represented by a little girl) and age (the man we assume to be her grandfather); closeness (the girl's family together at Christmas) and loneliness (the grandfather, viewed through a telescope, far away on the moon); the greyness of Christmas Day for the grandfather and then the joy of a gift arriving on balloons; the gift itself being an antidote to loneliness – a telescope allowing the granddaughter and old man to wave to each other at Christmas. The scene is portrayed under a line (which itself presumes they're *not* feeling loved):

> Show someone they're loved this Christmas.

BANKSY'S 'FLOWER BOMBER'

The unforgettable artwork 'Flower Bomber' (as it's been dubbed) by the street artist Banksy (google it for a reminder) draws its power of contrast from one image: a street rioter about to launch what one expects to be a rock or Molotov cocktail, but holding instead a bunch of flowers. Judyth Hill's poem 'Wage Peace' (written after the terror attacks of September 11, 2001) has been linked to Banksy's art for its similar contrast, in word form, between opposites.

TWO TYPES OF CONTRAST

Contrast is key. It helps the Centre Brain of your listeners to absorb and evaluate your 'ask', and come to a decision. Whenever I make a direct fundraising ask, I will always offer two choices which contrast with each other in some way. This helps shift the question from 'Should I respond?' to 'Which option should I respond to?'

There are two kinds of contrast.

THE GOOD CONTRASTED WITH THE LESS GOOD (OR BAD)

This route starts with asking yourself: what's the opposite of this? A popular phrase when I was a teenager captures this idea:

> Be there, or be square.

It's worth noting that this approach can be manipulative and needs some careful thinking. I heard of a sketch once in which a door-to-door salesman rings the bell and the homeowner opens the door:

> SALESMAN Do you want Richard to go blind? [*The salesman has brought 'Richard' with him – he's standing alongside on the doorstep.*]
> HOMEOWNER Er . . . well, no, of course not!
> SALESMAN Well, if you give £10, he won't. He has an eye disease which can be halted with an immediate donation of £10.

Humorous, perhaps, but in fact just an exaggerated version of what often happens. This approach can also disguise itself more subtly. For example:

> Would you babysit for us tonight? We haven't been out together for months; we desperately need time to talk.

In fact, if you're not able to babysit, I think our marriage may be in jeopardy!

THE TWO-ROUTES APPROACH

I have a friend, Richard, who's contracted an eye disease. We're raising money to help treat it and were wondering if you'd be willing to make a donation of £5. Or £10?

Would you be able to babysit tonight? Or, if not, perhaps another evening some time in the next few weeks?

I spent years working as a copywriter. One of the rules in writing sales copy is that if everything is a great deal, then, in fact, *nothing* is a great deal. The seller sets the benchmark and the buyer is persuaded, or not, based on the contrast that is offered.

The popular obsession in the UK with the weather follows similar rules: in October, when temperatures fall to 12° C, people comment on how cold it's getting. When, in January, temperatures rise from 1° to 12°, people comment on the fact that it's really warming up.

Most of the appeals made by charities I work with are built on contrast. What is unacceptable in one place may be seen as adequate in another. It depends on what you contrast it with. After the Second World War, when everyone was on rations and some didn't have enough to eat, asking a family to donate money to feed poor communities overseas might have been less warmly received than it is today. What's changed is contrast – between our level of need and theirs. And that contrast becomes our prompt to help.

The same principles apply to what makes discounted offers so popular and effective as a selling tool. Look at so-called Black Friday. Or the 6 a.m. queues for the 'Next sale after Christmas'. If you needed shoes, not desperately, but could do with some new ones, contrast might swing it for you: you see a discounted pair, marked down by £30. All that's happening in your Centre Brain is that you're allowing the seller to set the benchmark your brain will use against a contrasting option; this means your Centre Brain contrasts the reduced price with the benchmark set by the seller.

So to use the power of contrast in your own persuasion, you need to identify what the contrast is to what you're trying to persuade someone about.

CONTRAST, URINE AND CAMPFIRES

I was at a festival, due to go on to the main stage and speak to an audience of 25,000 people. The problem was that I was on stage immediately after a music band had finished their set, which was when people legged it to the toilets and burger vans. Having watched the stage speaker the day before, I knew she'd had to battle to keep the crowd's attention. I knew what I had to do: provide contrast. By filling both 'ends' of the scales in people's brains with something to weigh and contrast, I'd prevent their brains introducing another option to contrast with listening to me, namely: 'Get to the hotdog stand.'

I walked on as the band finished. I could see the edges of the huge crowd beginning to move, so I skipped the small talk and went for the contrast:

At this festival last year, on a sunny afternoon, around our campfire, something happened that made me want to vomit.

I knew I had the chance to hook people, so began to solidify this interest quickly. I followed with a question:

Who's seen the episode of Bear Grylls in the Wild where he drinks his own urine?

Hands go up. I sense people are engaging. Starting to wonder where the story is going . . .

My son is Bear's biggest fan. He wants to be Bear. We'd watched the 'urine' episode the week before we came to this festival. Copying Bear, he popped into our bell tent with a bottle like this . . .

I held up a replica of the bottle used.

. . . and filled it with his urine. He went to his little sister and said, 'Poppy, I've made you a drink.' She took it, and gulped down the contents. My son, feeling he'd now become Bear Grylls (though not quite clocking that Bear drank the urine himself rather than giving it to a defenceless four-year-old), was shocked at what happened next.

I had the crowd. It felt like all 25,000 people were listening . . .

The first we knew of it was when Poppy came charging over and shouted, 'He's given me wee to drink!', and

> began to vomit around the area where we were stand-
> ing with friends.

What I actually wanted to say – and was there to talk about – was a hunger crisis in West Africa which the audience could help solve. But to many festivalgoers, people there to enjoy music and fun, I knew this would sound worthy but dull. So I used all the Centre Brain's prompts: I'd painted a picture: a child swallowing something awful. I'd introduced an idea: something happened that made me want to vomit. And I presented the Why:

> What parent would intentionally give children they love
> something to eat or drink which would make you want
> to vomit? I met a woman last month who was doing just
> that. She loved her kids so much she was giving them
> items scavenged from the ground. That was the only
> food available. And, having lost one of her family to
> hunger, this woman was doing everything to keep her
> children alive.

The action centre had been prompted. Afterwards, the members of our team offering festivalgoers a chance to respond told me that people were coming up to *them* asking to get involved.

CONTRAST AS A BRAIN-PROMPT

In March 1993 photographer Kevin Carter was in South Sudan. He arrived at the village of Ayod on a United Nations food plane. While the parents of an emaciated Sudanese toddler collected food items from the aircraft, Carter went to photograph their little girl who was sitting in the dust. A vulture sat several metres from the girl. Carter later explained that he waited 20 minutes but the vulture didn't fly away. So he took a photograph that became a deeply iconic image – one the *New York Times* called a 'metaphor for Africa's despair'.[1] The contrast in the image was what made it immensely powerful: a wasting child (apparently close to death) watched by a waiting vulture. The child on its own, or vulture on its own, wouldn't have been as persuasive, but put them together . . .

Steve Jobs rightly pointed out that the best creative ideas come from connecting together, or synthesizing, two ideas:

> Creativity is just connecting things. When you ask creative people how they did something, they feel a little guilty because they didn't really do it, they just saw something. It seemed obvious to them after a while. That's because they were able to connect experiences they've had and synthesize new things.[2]

One of my favourite books is a 1969 copy of *Creative Person and Creative Process*, which is full of the findings of Dr Frank Barron, a psychologist who specialized in creativity. In the 1960s he invited a group of highly creative and well-known individuals to live together while he observed and conducted experiments. One method in his book is called Synectics. The word means the joining of different, apparently irrelevant elements. Or, in Dr Barron's words, 'making the strange familiar and the familiar strange'.[3] This approach is one of the best ways to identify strong ideas, using contrast, which prompt the Centre Brain.

Chapter 12 outlines how you can use contrast, not only as a prompt for influencing others, but also as a prompt for your own brain.

'MAY YOU HAVE A MIND
THAT LOVES FRONTIERS SO
THAT YOU CAN EVOKE THE
BRIGHT FIELDS THAT LIE
BEYOND THE VIEW OF THE
REGULAR EYE.'

— JOHN O'DONOHUE

6 The picture-power principle

Persuasive prompt 4: pictorialize your points

'If I say "sausage" your Centre Brain immediately conjures that picture for you.'

My daughter Poppy, in her first term at school, came home one day worried that she was about to become a jacket potato. She was deeply concerned. It turned out that her teacher, in trying to encourage Poppy to choose something different from the lunch menu, had said (as Poppy *again* chose the jacket potato option), 'Oh Poppy, you'll look like a jacket potato soon!' Poppy was worried. 'Now everyone thinks I'm going to become a jacket potato,' she told us.

The teacher's words had power in Poppy's mind because they were immediately visualized – turned into a picture – in her brain. She could see what she'd look like as a potato. And it freaked her out.

Pictures equal power in the Centre Brain. They grab attention, because they're the language the brain speaks, understands and responds to.

When my 18-year-old self learned French on the streets of Belgium it was, I realized, the pictures I used which enabled my brain to pick up French so much faster than I did at school. And to start thinking in it. Every week I'd knock on hundreds of front doors armed with a page of themed images. One week it might be foods in the kitchen. I wouldn't look up, or memorize, the words for each picture beforehand. Language helpers would go through the pictures with me on the doorstep. Others would invite me into their kitchens to show me the foods. I was learning as a child learns its mother tongue – by connecting the pictures seen to the words I was hearing spoken.

Some pictures are created by your Centre Brain (what you might call your 'mind's eye') in response to words you hear. If I say 'sausage' your Centre Brain immediately conjures that picture for you. Other pictures come through your physical eyes – what you see – absorbed from the outside world by your Centre Brain. Recent brain–imaging research from Eastern Illinois University has shown that when blind people read Braille the same neural circuitry is activated as it is for a sighted person: the visual cortex. Pictures are formed in the 'mind's eye', if not the visual eye.[1]

Where the picture comes from is less important than what it can do once it's in the Centre Brain.

Knowing that pictures jump-start the Centre Brain (which is itself the body's action centre or control room), the first step to unleashing your power of persuasion is to ask yourself: how much am I using pictures when I want to persuade? And are the pictures I use likely to draw people to my point or away from it?

YOUNG AND BEAUTIFUL?

When I worked in TV there was a frequently used mantra:

> Young is better than old; beautiful is better than ugly.

Apparently, it was right: viewing figures reflect people's preference for watching the young and beautiful over the old or ugly. Or, more correctly, the more engaged people are in a picture, the more it will influence their actions or viewing habits.

Pictures and visual images define and steer preference and reaction. Former MP Geoffrey Dickens apparently proved the point when attending a summer fete. A woman he later described as 'very ugly' asked for his autograph. He invited her to drop him a note at the House of Commons, and she did so, requesting a photograph of Mr Dickens. Intriguingly, she added the word 'Horseface' in brackets next to her name in the letter.

The MP later wrote,

> Filled with admiration for the way in which she had come to terms with her repulsive looks, I entered into the spirit of things. With a felt-tipped pen I wrote on the photograph 'To My Dear Friend Horseface – Love and Best Wishes, Geoffrey Dickens.' After it was safely in the post and on the way to my courageous constituent, my secretary informed me that she had been extremely helpful in writing Horseface after her name in case I had forgotten the lady in question.[2]

The woman's looks – the visual image – had dominated the MP's memory of her because, for the Centre Brain, pictures are the mother tongue. Think about a double-decker bus. Now recall the room you awoke in today. Finally, bring your mum to mind. Your Centre Brain on receiving these instructions has revealed its mother tongue by showing you pictures. You saw an *image* of a bus, not the *word* 'bus', because images are your brain's normal operating language. This is true in one's waking life as well as in sleep, where dreams are a result of your Centre Brain processing pictures.

THE PICTURE-POWER PRINCIPLE

When you run into someone from a year or two ago and say, 'I know your face, but your name's just escaping me', you're experiencing the difference between the Centre Brain's ability to hold on to pictures (the person's face) over the long term compared to your Outer Brain's relatively weak capacity for storing one-off words (the person's name). To remember words for the long term, your Outer Brain needs the help of the Centre Brain. Try associating a word or name you think you'll forget with a picture and you'll find your ability to recall the word will increase by up to 800 per cent. (For example, if you're forgetting the name of your new friend Brad, picture Brad Pitt and associate the two.)

So how is it we manage to store words at all if the language area of our brain leaves us struggling to remember new words – and demanding intentional effort to learn them – while the picture area of the brain seems to hold on to the images it sees without much intentional effort? At school I was learning French with words, asking my Outer Brain to memorize oodles of new words, and failing. In Belgium, however, I used pictures to learn the words, and, as the story in Chapter 1 explains, I was thinking in the language in six weeks.

This principle of picture-power is the Centre Brain's fourth prompt to action: give it a picture and you have the power to prompt a response. And to do this you need to start by pictorializing all your points (Chapter 13 provides a technique for doing this).

It *is* possible to learn a language by using your conscious Outer Brain (with the exception of foreign exchanges and conversation classes, this is how my children are learning Spanish at school right now), but you will be slow to master it and you'll forget it quite fast. But learn it through the subconscious Centre Brain and you'll speak and read at speed. Right now, you're only able to read these words as fast as you are doing because you're absorbing the words as pictures.

Assuming you're an experienced reader, your Centre Brain will treat the words you read as pictures. Instead of spelling out each word (as a new reader would), the Centre Brain provides the pronunciation of the words at a subconscious speed, by treating them as pictures. The brain refers to its 'visual dictionary', where the 'look' of each word is stored as a picture or visual object. Drawing on these images enables fast reading.[3] And it means that each word is far more than just a collection of letters with a meaning. Words carry wider associations from the Centre Brain. This is how your brain can so efficiently build a 'mind's-eye' picture of a story as you read it.

When you read that gripping fiction book, the words you read are brushstrokes for your Centre Brain to create the picture. They carry the details from which your brain creates a visualization of the story. These images can be so real that if you later see a film based on the book, it can feel 'incorrect' in its depiction of the locations and characters – because they don't match your brain's own pictorialization.

SHARKS, TOASTERS AND T. REXES

Nelson Mandela said, 'If you talk to a man in a language he understands, that goes to his head. If you talk to him in his language, that goes to his heart.'[4]

Dr Lynell Burmark is an author and expert on visual literacy. She says:

> Unless our words, concepts, ideas are hooked onto an image, they will go in one ear, sail through the brain, and go out the other ear. Words are processed by our short-term memory where we can only retain about seven bits of information . . . Images, on the other hand, go directly into long-term memory where they are indelibly etched.[5]

Research carried out by Reuters journalist and blogger Alister Doyle revealed that although sharks killed nine people in the year he was writing, faulty toasters killed a staggering 791 people. Doyle blogged that despite knowing the facts, the image of the shark seemed to retain control of his emotions: 'I can't shake off being more frightened of sharks than toasters', he wrote.[6]

This is because his Centre Brain uses images and pictures to direct action. And, because the picture it holds of sharks is a bloody one, no amount of logical information, or statistics, will change this. The Outer Brain handles logic, and though it may conclude that toasters are to be feared more than sharks, this will remain a conclusion, unable to prompt action. It's the Centre Brain, prompted by pictures, that will determine the individual's response – which is to avoid sharks more than toasters.

This means that points which are not pictorialized will lack power to prompt action, instead leading only to conclusions. Only a picture, whether in front of you or in your mind's eye, will stimulate action.

I could tell my wife that a Tyrannosaurus rex is coming, charging round the corner at her, and she'd reach a conclusion: well, it will be a costume, with a person inside it. Nothing to worry about. Yet one day, when the actual image *appeared* round the corner, it did prompt action. We were at the brilliant Eden Project, Cornwall, at the time.

We came upon the beast as it emerged from a large tent. It was both realistic and big. Its tooth-lined jaws opened, emitting a realistic roar. Even a watching dog barked at it and backed off. The only indication of its humanity was a small section of the legs of the operator hidden inside, visible from a certain angle.

As it ran towards my youngest son, he fled. My daughter dived into the arms of her mum. 'It's OK,' I said. 'Look down there – you can see the legs of the person inside: it's only a costume.' (On reflection this was a well-intended but entirely unhelpful comment for a four-year-old!)

My wife said she felt her pulse rate rising and instinctively ran when it roared towards her.

As the main language of your brain, pictures provide the evidence to prompt decisions – to run, to stand still, to smile, to cry, to kiss, to buy. They're the main operating language for your action brain.

This piece of knowledge may mean it's the right time to revisit that 'bolted door' you'd thought was shut to you for good – the client who was resistant to the style of persuasion you'd been deploying.

When Walt Disney began building Disney World, Florida, he had Cinderella's castle erected first. He wanted to motivate and stir the builders and other visitors as they arrived each day with this picture of what was coming, to inspire them. As Disney himself said: 'Of all of our inventions for mass communication, pictures still speak the most universally understood language.'[7]

Something called the 'picture superiority effect' confirms this: in our brains, images will always outperform words as prompts for the brain. What this means is seismic.

But hang on a minute! Aren't stories the key to great communication? It's true that stories do often prompt the Centre Brain to emotion and response – but only because they paint a *picture* in the mind of the listener. And pictures are among the main prompts for the brain.

A VILLAGE IN FLAMES

My eight-year-old son Aidan and I had been warmly welcomed into a remote, rural community in Uganda. And what we saw there stuck.

On our first evening, we helped a family find dinner – at a termite hill. Sitting by a six-foot-high termite mound, our African friends inserted lengths of grass down holes and drew out the insects; this was their only meal that evening.

On our second afternoon, some members of the community re-enacted for us the events of a day four years previously, when rebels surrounded their village. An army of child soldiers. A village in flames. They even ignited a purpose-built thatched hut to add realism.

Early next morning, I saw Aidan at the village borehole, with new friend Holly, struggling to copy her as she carried on her head a container filled with 20 litres of water.

These moments remain. Stored in my head. They are there because a part of my Centre Brain known as the 'hippocampus' (think of it as your brain's camera) captures and stores key moments as pictures, building a library which the Centre Brain then refers to constantly to help it make decisions.

It was our last night in that village, and Jim, a gentle, large-framed man of around 70 who'd been born in that place – and four years later would die there – lit the fire.

Villagers emerged from the darkness to sit around the furnace. Children, old people, teenagers, mums and dads.

'This', Jim told me, 'has happened here for the past 70 years. Many of our people cannot read or write but they learn the stories we tell around the fire.'

We felt privileged to be invited into what felt like a sacred event that evening.

One story told of the day the villagers returned after the rebels' departure – finding nothing but tumbled mud huts, slaughtered cattle, and bodies. Another told of how the village church began under the mango tree.

Every child's birth – and name – had a story. We'd seen each morning how, as the women pounded millet, their songs told stories. And round the fire, that night, a new generation of children saw each story come to life in pictures, in their brains, as it was told.

Where I'm from, the idea of entrusting a community's history, going back years, to residents' memories would seem risky. Rely instead on digital storage, with backups; even write the history in a book. Surely the Centre Brain can't hold on to images for *that* long?

The Independent reported a story that suggests it can. An Ethiopian farmer, Dhaqabo Ebba, clearly recalls images and pictures that suggest he is around 160 years old.[8] He recalls different government leaders, and his recollections – all in picture form – of historical events and the people in his own family tree do point to Mr Ebba being the world's oldest man! Whether he's 160 or not, what is accepted is that people in old age, particularly when dementia sets in, often begin to recall with great clarity scenes from their early life. Pictures are the vehicle our brains use to write our life narrative in. Anything vital is logged in them. To try to be persuasive without them is like trying to dig a hole in compacted earth with a comb – and wondering why you're making slow progress.

BUT HANG ON . . .

At this point you may be recalling a time when you persuaded sceptical listeners – without using pictures or visual metaphors – to reach, even embrace, a conclusion they'd previously resisted. Conclusions, though, don't inevitably lead to action, and they are housed in a very different part of the brain from the centres leading to action.

The Outer Brain specializes in conclusions, because it advises the Centre Brain and leaves that region to decide to act or not. It doesn't go further. I have sat in many meetings with clients in which they persuade their directors of something. Often statistics and logical analysis are used to drive this. The conclusion is reached but, importantly, is not connected to any action. Months of further discussions may follow as to whether action should be taken around the theoretical agreement obtained.

That's when pictures are most needed: they will awaken and connect with the action-focused Centre Brain. Data, statistics, logical argument will land in the Outer Brain and prompt a conclusion only. Without pictorializing these words, you'll find action harder to generate.

The advertisers at Volvo knew this when they ran what became a hugely successful campaign, winning them dominance in the safe-car brand territory. Their 'Cages Save Lives' commercials showed a cage protecting a diver from sharks that were ramming into it. For parents wanting the best protection for their children, the idea visualized the message 'Volvos have the Impact Protection System' into a persuasive call to act.

Do you fancy a long, dry, edible item, sliced down the centre, covered in sticky stuff and with a fluffy white ingredient on top? That's the words version, and as you read your Outer Brain is searching for a way to visualize it and work it out in pictorial form so that you can decide. How about a cream bun with icing and fresh cream all the way through? That's the picture version. Your Centre Brain can decide, using the image, whether you fancy one.

A Greek friend often uses a phrase from his home town: 'We eat with our eyes first.' Long before the cream bun reaches your lips, the image has prompted action: saliva and a sudden urge to consume the treat. The words version won't do that.

Pictorializing your point speeds up communication. Today in our age of digital communications, more information will hit you than would have been the case, doing the same activity, 30 years ago. As a result, the bits of information that do get through have had to work harder than ever before.

When you communicate without using pictures – or any of the other prompts in this book – it feels like this to your audience:

> Think about a curved line with every point equal from the centre.

That word-description alone prompts the processing machinery in your Outer Brain to begin trying to form a picture from that description – to then feed it to the Centre Brain. But if you speak directly to the Centre Brain you need just two words to give the brain the picture it seeks from that description:

> A circle.

A LIBRARY IN YOUR HEAD

In Part 3 you can see examples of several successful leaders whose words, still remembered and quoted today, use imagery not as a one-off but to build an experience for their audience. And the stronger the picture your brain forms, the more it will influence your listeners' behaviour *into the future*. This is because your Centre Brain uses pictures in two ways: 1) they prompt action now, and 2) they're given a place in your brain's visual library, which your brain draws on every day to guide key decisions.

Bring to mind a friend. Any friend. And notice how, around the edges of your thinking, your brain is offering you associated images. Try this with several different friends or family members. Or places you've been. Or key moments in your life. When you think of such a person or place, your Centre Brain will access its visual library and bring to mind other mutual friends, or linked images of situations you were in together. Or events that occurred in the location you're recalling.

This means that if you want to build a case for something, restating the facts won't help. If, instead, you find ways to offer pictures and images to members of your audience, their brains will begin to build – or add to – a collection of images on that issue, which they then draw on to guide decisions subconsciously.

This is how 'lovemarks', as Kevin Roberts calls them, are created. Lovemarks are brands which Roberts describes as attracting 'loyalty beyond reason'.[9] It's because those brands have managed to add images of their product, and the experience it offers, to the image libraries in the brains of purchasers that they win a level of loyalty from the Centre Brain which is beyond the reason of the Outer Brain.

GROWING THEIR VISUAL VAULT

The British Library is the world's largest. It's home to over 170 million books, and growing weekly. An online encyclopedia, Wikipedia, has over five million articles and the number increases by around 20,000 every month.

What goes on in the heads of your listeners, when you speak to their Centre Brain with pictures, loosely reflects the constant adding to the British Library and Wikipedia. Pictures are added daily to the visual library of the hippocampus of every person in your audience. The question is: are *your* images among those being added to *their* visual library? And what part will adding images play in persuading them?

Imagine the Centre Brain of each individual in your audience as being like a huge visual vault – a vault which isn't just a store, but is also a constant reference: informing, guiding and deciding which course of action to take.

If you're a lover of Coke, chances are that Pepsi is always your second choice of soft drink, and vice versa. The reason? It has less to do with the actual taste than you might think. Research in the journal *Neuron* has revealed how the visual memories which your Centre Brain associates with tastes strongly influence how you act in response to a choice. In other words, if you're oblivious to which drink you have in your hand, you're likely to be happy with either Pepsi or Coke. But see a visual cue of the Coke branding and the hippocampus will activate its stored images and influence how you act – which drink you choose.[10]

When you face any situation today, your Centre Brain will decide what to do by reviewing – at lightning speed – related images it has stored in its visual library. The Centre Brain processes pictures 60,000 times faster than words.[11] This is how, as Malcolm Gladwell's book *Blink* explains, humans are able to make largely accurate judgements in the blink of an eye. 'Whenever we meet someone for the first time,' he writes, 'whenever we react to a new idea, whenever we're faced with making a decision quickly and under stress, we use that second part of the brain.'[12] This 'second part' is the part described here as the Centre Brain.

In persuasion terms, this is where the power of persuasive communication is unleashed in both the present and the future. Pictorialize your point and speak to the part of the brain in a language able to mobilize it to action. And also earn the picture a place in the brain's image reference library, so that the next time your listener considers a related decision – let's say you were convincing him or her of how nice a certain brand of soup is – your image will be one of those which the Centre Brain references to reach a decision, and he or she will choose that brand again.

When you walk in snow, you create footprints, and these prints freeze over after a day or two of icy weather. It's a similar process when you plant a picture in the Centre Brain: it remains, and retains the message, feeling and momentum it brought, so that every time it's referenced, its persuasive power is also at play.

I'M 80 BUT FEEL 21

The larger your visual library becomes, the greater the fodder at your fingertips when communicating. In neuroscience it's a sort of snowballing effect. The more neurons talk to other neurons, the stronger they become. And they talk more when they're used. This process is called 'long-term potentiation'. It means that your image-library – and that of your listener – can keep growing. Perhaps this explains why, in traditional Chinese culture, birthdays are not a big thing until a person reaches 60. Old age is revered, partly because, as Plato put it, 'the spiritual eyesight improves as the physical eyesight declines'.[13]

Put another way, while we're in our teenage years we experience an excess of energy and hunger, but we lack the extensive library of images to guide us in our actions and choices. In older age our subconscious brain gives us better guidance as it draws on a much larger picture-library – though sometimes without the energy.

I once met world-renowned theologian John Stott who, in 2005, had been declared by *Time* magazine to be one of the 100 most influential people in the world. He told me that every morning he looked in the mirror and was shocked at seeing an old man, because inside he still felt as if he was 21.

If you want to stay young inside – to grow up without growing old – you need to ensure your Centre Brain picture-library doesn't get overstocked with images of safe or mundane experiences. Because when it does, when it gets used to and adjusts to the mundane, it will prompt you to *seek* the mundane. Such an imbalance will dampen your subconscious brain's appetite for living on the wild side (whatever that means for you).

It's no coincidence that Bear Grylls, 18 months after breaking his back while jumping from a helicopter, tackled Mount Everest, obtaining a place in the *Guinness Book of Records*. What drove this action? His Centre Brain picture-library had been well stocked with pictures and associated emotions of exploratory, outdoor experiences. And these prompted more of the same.

This means that, for your persuasive communication, your choice of pictures needs to strike a balance: suiting your audience in terms of their current situation, and tempting them towards whatever action you are seeking to convince them of.

ENGAGED BY A CRUCIFIXION

Research has shown that *seeing* generates longer-lasting memory than *hearing*.[14] At the Salzburg Festival in 1928, Helen Tamiris, the famous American pioneer of modern dance, performed a gripping contemporary dance piece, set to the spiritual folk song 'Crucifixion', performed by the New English Orchestra. The words of the song alone, without dance, paint a fairly graphic picture:

> They crucified my Lord
> An' he never said a mumbling word.

> They nailed him to a tree
> An' he never said a mumbling word.

> They pierced him in the side
> An' he never said a mumblin' word.

> The blood came twinklin' down
> An' he never said a mumblin' word.[15]

But I was chilled when I *saw* the dance. It was 1998. My wife, a dancer herself, was performing the piece with several other dancers on the *Jedermann* stage as part of the Salzburg Festival, on the anniversary of its performance there by Helen Tamiris 70 years earlier.

The dance haunted everyone. I can see it now, two decades later: the dancers forming almost inhuman, pointed shapes and movements in response to the 1928 choreography which had instructed 'stabs and jiggles – the piercing of the nails and thorns'.[16]

Pictures absorbed by the Centre Brain prompt emotion. And lead to response. If the picture you paint, through your communication, is engaging and generates a warm emotional connection, it will prompt an active, engaged response. If the picture you communicate is frightening and doesn't connect through the emotion it conjures up, it will prompt disengagement.

But this doesn't mean that pictorializing for persuasion requires *only* warm, inviting images that prompt fuzzy emotion. Pictures of jeopardy and struggle can be as persuasive as pictures that present hope and opportunity. Any picture can be persuasive if the communicator builds in the connection.

CONNECTION

The 'Crucifixion' dance at the Salzburg Festival is a good example of a particularly brutal picture (a murder) that somehow engaged people in an emotional response. In the words of my wife, Ruth, who danced it:

> We were trying to give the audience a moving picture of Christ being nailed to the cross, and on the cross as he suffered. A picture of the pain, through movement. The choreography was sharp, tight and rigid. Very serious and very strong. Dancing it, we were trying to feel the pain through our movements, to feel the pain of the event so that the audience could also feel it.

So why did people stay? As the dance promoted the emotion and pain of crucifixion, and the story of piercings and blood flowing was sung in the spiritual song, why did the picture draw lengthy applause and not a mass exodus?

Even when a film makes you weep, you come out stirred, having enjoyed the emotional connection. When a friend shares heart-breaking news, you don't run; you embrace them. When I worked for the UK TV channel GMTV, we set up a fake mugging on the South Bank, London, near the London TV Centre. There had been a story of a 'have-a-go hero' and we were testing how will-ing people were to get involved if they happened to witness a crime. The cameras were hidden as the first actor – an old lady with a walking stick – set out towards an unsuspecting member of the public coming the other way. Actor number two – a rough-looking young man – grabbed the old lady's bag just as the member of the public was within reach of them. He shook the handbag and, on cue, a heap of coins fell out, clattering to the ground. The old woman looked at the passing stranger and called out for his help. Seven out of the ten passers-by stepped in and grabbed the 'mugger' (at some risk to themselves), or attempted to stop him taking the handbag.

The factor that swings how the Centre Brain of your listeners responds to the pictures you show is the presence of emotional connection. Even in the face of a 'mugger', physically smaller people stepped in because the picture before them had enabled connection with the old lady.

Emotional connection is what can make a picture – any picture – powerful and persuasive.

'HE IS A BORE. A TERRIBLE, THUMPING, GROUND-SHUDDERING T. REX OF A BORE . . . AT THE END HIS VOICE ROSE TO AN ANGRY SHOUT. BUT OF COURSE THAT IS THE BORE'S FALL-BACK. IF YOU CAN'T ROUSE EMOTION IN OTHER PEOPLE, PRETEND TO CREATE IT IN YOURSELF.'

– SIMON HOGGART,
HOUSE OF FUN

7 The emotional-connection principle

Persuasive prompt 5: emotional connection makes it matter

'If the rational, Outer Brain response is like Blu Tack – generating a short-term hold – so emotional connection is like welding.'

What drives you to buy a product when you know a parallel product would do the same job at half the price? 'Loyalty beyond reason', as Kevin Roberts calls it,[1] is what does this. It's the Centre Brain flexing its muscles and acting because of a connection, in spite of the Outer Brain's rational, and contrary, conclusion that the alternative product is cheaper. That loyalty is forged by the Centre Brain's fifth prompt to action: emotional connection.

As Blaise Pascal put it, in *De L'Art de persuader*: 'People almost invariably arrive at their beliefs not on the basis of proof but on the basis of what they find attractive.'[2]

The Centre Brain of the person or people you're communicating with *wants* to connect. This is at the heart of why the Centre

Brain prompts work so effectively. The brain is designed to connect. It seeks connection. Emotional connection. And mirror neurons are what enable this connection.

Mirror neurons are what your Centre Brain uses to 'bring in' what it sees in others, to mirror, reflect and empathize, in order to connect. When you feel tears coming to your eyes while a friend tells you a tragic story; when you feel anger rising as a colleague explains that he or she is the victim of an apparent injustice, it's your mirror neurons mirroring, in you, the experience that you see or hear about. This is at the heart of emotional connection.

EMOTIONAL CONNECTION = ACTION

Emotional connection engages the brain's action centre.

Football is about emotional connection. It can turn watching parents, who've never met, into brothers and sisters as the shared commitment to the game creates these bonds. The same emotion may also lead to trouble: in a recent email sent to the parents of children playing in my son's 'footy league', the managers introduced some new rules

> because of a number of serious incidents and a whole host of ongoing issues with referees being intimidated . . .

If you support a team, you'll understand the significant part that your attendance and support plays, emotionally. The sense of shared identity, comradeship and connection is tangible.

Gareth Bale, the Real Madrid winger and Welsh team forward, trademarked the brilliant 'heart sign' celebration in which he forms the shape of a heart with his fingers, over his chest, when scoring a goal. The press has suggested it dates back to 2010 when Bale first made the gesture as an emotional sign to his partner Emma Rhys-Jones. In 2014 it found its way into the sellout FIFA video games, where it still appears. It's one of a substantial assortment of emotional connectors which reflect the depth of people's commitment in football.

If you drive a car, you'll have first-hand experience of a large emotional-connection area on the steering wheel. It's called the hooter! It may express warm emotion – hooting at a friend as you drive past, or anger as another driver cuts in front of your vehicle. But both forge connection.

Of the five prompts that awaken the brain's action centre, this one – emotional connection – is the most pervasive. It's everywhere.

MOMENT BY MOMENT

Whenever you throw money into the cup of a homeless man, it's because something stuck with you – maybe you glanced at the hole in his shoes, or saw him rubbing his hands together to warm them as the frost came down, or read his sign: 'Money for hot soup please'. Emotional connection is created by a specific insight, and leads to a specific response.

The first four Centre Brain prompts – ideas; answering why; using contrast; pictures – all help to create this emotional connection, to frame the situation or insight which will prompt the connection. Emotional connection happens daily, hourly and – as the examples below show – not just with people. You'll see that they are all the result of one of the Centre Brain prompts; they all result in emotional connection to a different thing and they all lead to action:

- You commission a builder to extend your house, having read a home-development magazine extolling the idea that your home can be the source of growing relationships with friends. The *idea* forms an emotional connection to stronger friendships in your area and leads you to arrange the extension.
- You decide to adopt a rescue dog after reading an article on the plight of growing numbers of abandoned pet dogs which answered *why* you should adopt one; this generated an emotional connection with the issue of neglected animals.
- You are prompted to throw a coin in the cup of a young homeless man after thinking about the *contrast* between the old homeless man you passed on a previous street and this younger person. This prompted an emotional connection to the opportunity this young man might have to escape a life on the streets.
- You choose to leave your job and start your own business, a decision which first took root when you saw *pictures* on social media of a peer who left his job, started a business and has had some success. This generated an emotional connection to the possibility of this sort of change.
- You make an impromptu decision to snap up a neighbour's old caravan when he upgrades to a better model; you are driven by the mental pictures you have visualized of his family's experiences each summer, which you hear of every year.

This purchase is the result of an *emotional connection* with an experience you foresee for yourself and your own family.

The fifth Centre Brain prompt therefore acts as oxygen to the first four prompts – giving life to them.

BUT I'M A RATIONAL THINKER!

As a persuasion prompt, it's important to remember that all human brains are wired to connect. Whether you see yourself as a rational thinker or an emotional connector has little bearing on the reality: your Centre Brain seeks emotional connection. And emotional connection is the oxygen which breathes life into your persuasiveness.

If you see feelings as fluffy, don't tar emotions with that same brush. They're not fluffy at all.

Emotions are a very different beast from feelings. If emotions are the puppet master, feelings are the puppet – responding to the lead of the emotions. In terms of origins, emotions originate in the Centre Brain (the action centre) and are physical. They prompt biochemical reactions which change you physically. In contrast, feelings come from the Outer Brain (the area specializing in gathering information to help you form conclusions). They can't be measured and are mental reactions *to* the emotion. Feelings are your Outer Brain saying, 'If that's the Centre Brain's emotional reaction to this situation, here are some feelings in response.'

So emotions, believe it or not, are what enable your rational style: you still experience them, but they may just be expressed at different levels in different ways physically.

When attempting to convince an individual or an audience of something (call this process 'marketing', 'persuasion', 'fundraising' – choose your own word), there is a constant drive within us to achieve an immediate result.

Analysing this drive, a recent IPA study, *The Long and the Short of It*, found that while rational messaging generates a short-term uplift in response (with no demonstrable change in sales), emotional priming generates a longer-term increase in response as well as growing the brand (or lasting emotional connection) by changing people's perceptions.[3]

My interpretation of these findings at the source – in the Centre Brain – says that if the rational, Outer Brain response is like Blu Tack – generating a short-term hold – so emotional connection is like welding, which brings together two things and melds them together, binding them tightly, generating long-term hold.

Therefore to be persuasive you must understand, embrace and *use* the immense power of emotion. It's important not to be misled into assuming that emotions have little impact or influence in the real world. The opposite is true.

RATIONAL ANALYTICS NEED EMOTION

The executives at Google, the masters of analytics, undertook a project, termed 'Project Aristotle', to determine what makes the perfect team. The *New York Times* reported on it like this:

> Google became focused on building the perfect team . . .
> The company's top executives long believed that building

the best teams meant combining the best people ... In 2012, the company embarked on an initiative – code-named Project Aristotle – to study hundreds of Google's teams and figure out why some stumbled while others soared. [Abeer] Dubey, a leader of the project, gathered some of the company's best statisticians, organizational psychologists, sociologists and engineers.

The study researched two types of teams. Team A included people

who are all exceptionally smart and successful ... who wait until a topic arises in which they are an expert, and then they speak at length ... This team is efficient. There is no idle chitchat or long debates. The meeting ends as scheduled and disbands ...

Team B runs very differently:

It's evenly divided between successful executives and middle managers with few professional accomplishments. Teammates jump in and out of discussions. People interject and complete one another's thoughts. When a team member abruptly changes the topic, the rest of the group follows him off the agenda. At the end of the meeting, the meeting doesn't actually end: Everyone sits around to gossip and talk about their lives.

What can Google tell us about the perfect team?

Perhaps surprisingly for an organization known for its analytics and data-driven success, the finding was rather Centre Brain:

Team B was more successful than Team A. The difference between the teams in terms of performance and success at task was how team members treated one another: whether people felt able to be themselves; whether everyone in the team had a chance to speak and contribute. Put another way, whether they felt emotionally connected. As *New York Times* reporter Charles Duhigg summarized:

> Human bonds matter as much at work as anywhere else . . . no one wants to put on a 'work face' when they get to the office. No one wants to leave part of their personality and inner life at home . . . We must be able to talk about what is messy or sad, to have hard conversations with colleagues who are driving us crazy. We can't be focused just on efficiency . . . We want to know that work is more than just labor . . . Success is often built on experiences – like emotional interactions and complicated conversations and discussions of who we want to be and how our teammates make us feel . . .[4]

THE POWER OF EMOTION

In the IPA study mentioned above, *The Long and the Short of It*, the researchers looked at the power of emotion within adverts to drive response (purchase) over the long term. It found that for an advert to form a lasting emotional connection it must relate to things the viewer cares about.

These findings confirm that lasting emotional connection breathes life into persuasiveness.

The study also found that emotional advertising is *twice as efficient* as rational advertising, and delivers twice the profit.

Your Centre Brain is brilliant at imitating, and uses this ability to build emotional connection. Techniques for building emotional connection draw on the other four Centre Brain prompts, leading to something I call a 'defining moment'.

HUMANITY WASHED UP

As the refugee crisis grew during 2015, the collective Outer Brain of the UK went into overdrive, prompting people to reach a conclusion, to find a position, on how to deal with migrants seeking to enter the UK: 'Am I keen to throw open the borders to fleeing Syrians (at one extreme), to close them (at the other) or am I somewhere in the middle?' As the facts were publicized around the number of refugees arriving on European shores, the Outer Brain responded to those facts and drew a conclusion.

One well-publicized 'vibe' in parts of the UK, pushed along by a large portion of the press, was to respond with fear at being overrun. This meant that while Germany took around 800,000 refugees in the year from June 2014 to 2015, and Lebanon saw its 4.5 million population swamped by 1.5 million refugees, the UK government responded to what then Prime Minister David Cameron described as 'a swarm of people' camped in Calais by taking in 166 Syrian refugees that same year.

The feeling of fear was driven by the Outer Brain's rational assessment of what it saw. Which begs the question: if the Centre

Brain is the decision-maker, the action centre, can it really over-come rational, thought-through conclusions?

The answer is yes, if emotion is deployed.

Emotion exists in the Centre Brain and speaks the language that prompts the Centre Brain to action. An emotional response to one boy's story was the prompt that awoke the Centre Brain of British people on the subject of refugees.

Aylan Kurdi was the boy's name. We'd heard facts about refugee children being washed up on Europe's shores. But when a picture emerged, the Centre Brain woke up and listened, and connection was generated. Aylan's small lifeless body was photographed washed up, face down, on a sandy beach. One newspaper which had previously referred to migrants as 'cockroaches' began a campaign in the boy's name: 'For Aylan'. The British prime minister agreed to accept 4,000 refugees a year – a large increase in comparison to the 166 admitted the previous year.

However clear someone is on an issue, an emotional response can still change his or her view, as it did for many people after Aylan's picture hit the press. Persuasion must use emotion.

But, as we all know, emotion works both ways – prompting generosity of spirit or anger. In 2006 the French footballer Zinedine Zidane had cross words with Marco Materazzi in the France–Italy World Cup Final. Emotion took control of Zidane: he headbutted Materazzi in the sternum and was 'red carded' by the referee. The match was important, and logically Zidane would have known a headbutt would see him sent off the pitch just when his country most needed him. So why on earth did he do it?

His logical, rational Outer Brain had been 'hijacked' and silenced by his Centre Brain, which was being driven to action by emotion. This is often termed an 'emotional hijack'; its biological name is an 'amygdala flood'. I prefer to describe its effects or impact, calling what happens a defining moment.

THE AMYGDALA FLOOD

The amygdala flood, or hijack, reveals the power the Centre Brain can exercise over the logic of the Outer Brain. The emotion that this flood releases is physical, making an impact on the human body in tangible ways. Tears are the most obvious, but other physical signs include flushing or going pale, deep breathing, sweating and many other subtle shifts.

Amygdala floods happen to us at significant moments. And, as well as being brought on *by* significant moments or events, they *create* significant moments in the action they prompt in us. They help to define who we are, our outlook and our actions.

Several years ago, my wife Ruth and I were sitting at home watching an annual, popular, celebrity-driven charity fundraiser on TV. Having made films in poor communities in many countries, I watched with an awareness of the importance of self-regulating – of giving space and honouring the dignity of people being filmed. This sometimes involves switching the camera off despite knowing how powerful the footage would be.

As we watched, a short film was played in which (as far as we could see) the cameraman was in the back of a Land Rover, opposite a mother. Her son had malaria and was dying. As they raced to the clinic, the child lost his fight, and died. On camera. We may have missed something – it may have been that the mother wanted their story told in full. But if so, that wasn't made clear. Ruth and I were appalled. Our rational Outer Brains were dissecting what we imagined had happened in that vehicle, and were faced with a clear conclusion: the producers should not have filmed that tragic event. Having concluded that we were appalled, we kept watching – perhaps evidence that the Outer Brain's conclusions don't prompt action. Despite the logic informing our disgust for how this charity appeared to operate, 25 minutes later we called up and donated, tears in our eyes.

What happened?

A second short film began, which spoke to our Centre Brains, and hijacked the previous conclusions of the Outer Brain. It prompted us to *act* in opposition to the rational conclusion offered by the Outer Brain.

The second film featured two children sitting alone, in the dark, round a small fire outside their family's mud-hut home, somewhere in Africa. In between sobs, the older child explained that their mum had just died (because of an AIDS-related infection) and their dad had died the previous year. They were all alone. The younger sibling wept as her brother spoke. I can confirm that my Centre Brain prompted an amygdala flood – a hijack – because of the clarity of the image it stored: even now, as I see the picture my visual library stored, I can feel a strong emotional connection to want to do something about that situation. And the effect of this flood was that it defined my commitment to children affected by HIV. It was, in that way, a defining moment.

PERMANENT PERSUASION

When your brain has an amygdala flood the hippocampus (the brain's camera) is prompted to capture a picture of the event. That picture is added to the Centre Brain's image-library which is used daily to help determine responses. Every time I think about making a donation to an HIV/AIDS or African children's charity, my brain brings back the image of those children.

That flood and the defining moment it creates defines your listeners' view of the issue you want to persuade them about. This is how you can influence someone not just once but many times, earning a more permanent place in a person's Centre Brain: achieving permanent persuasion.

It's this that explains 'lovemarks' – the name Kevin Roberts gives to products and brands that attract 'loyalty beyond reason'.[5] That loyalty and love starts with a defining emotional experience. Or, in Centre Brain terms, an amygdala flood.

The negative consequences which amygdala floods can prompt are better known than the positive opportunities they also offer. Think of Zidane's headbutt (Zidane never returned to the field as a player). The imprint that an amygdala flood leaves on the Centre Brain is greater than the imprint left by normal daily interactions involving the Centre Brain. And this positive persuasive-potential is waiting to be harnessed.

THE DEFINING MOMENT

Your Outer Brain operates a little like a tidal-zone beach; that's a beach on which all the sand goes under the sea at high tide (i.e. is 'in' the tidal zone) and is again accessible at low tide. Every day, events, activities, conversations are like a tide clearing information from your brain, coming in, going out. This is how the brain manages the mass of information it receives.

We holiday at a tidal beach every year and enjoy using buckets and spades to make various structures in the sand. But no matter how big or impressive the sandcastle, or beach labyrinth (last year's build of choice), when you return the next day, it's gone.

If the beach is your audience's brain, how do you make what you communicate stand the test of the regular tide? How can you earn a place for what you communicate in the minds of those in your audience?

Think about last weekend, and of three people you spoke with: what did you discuss? If you can remember, it's because the Centre Brain prompts were part of that bit of the conversation. (Was there an idea, a Why, a contrast or a picture with some level of emotional connection?) They're the only means of retaining what happened in the face of the constant flow of information that washes in and out.

The five Centre Brain prompts make your communication like a football-sized rock on a tidal-zone beach. When the tide goes out, it retains its place.

My family and I often drag big rocks over to our sandcastles in the tidal zone, and they're still there the next morning. The Outer Brain information is like what's been drawn or written in the sand – it's washed away with the next tide. But the rock holds its place. Nevertheless, by next year even those football-sized rocks are gone.

This is how the Centre Brain makes space: by replacing similar memories with more up-to-date ones. This isn't you *losing* important memories, but updating them. Imagine you cycle into town daily and each day park your bike in a different place; your brain has to replace these memories, or you'd spend hours each day unable to distinguish between last week's memory of where you left your bike and today's.

Also on our holiday beach are several huge, bus-sized boulders. The sort that even a fork-lift truck would struggle to shift. They stay, year on year. They've earned their place, and although altered by the sea, they remain very present and visible, influencing how the beach is seen.

You can make your communications resemble one of those big boulders on the sand, by generating a defining moment. This means they will be there tomorrow, next week, next year.

If the tidal beach represents the brain of the person you're persuading, then:

- Communicating from – and to – the Outer Brain with facts and 'what and how' information is like writing in the sand: it will be gone tomorrow.

- Communicating from – and to – the Centre Brain using ideas, the Why, contrast, pictures and emotion is like placing a football-sized rock on the sand: it will be there tomorrow. By next year it may be covered by sand, and less obvious, but it will always be there.
- Communicating from – and to – the Centre Brain using ideas, the Why, contrast, pictures and emotion, and using these to create a defining moment, is like dropping a bus-sized boulder on to the sand. It's going to stay there, changing the view and defining the outlook into the future.

DEFINING MOMENTS OF A GENERATION

My parents, and most in their generation, talk of recalling exactly where they were when they heard of the assassination of US President John F. Kennedy in 1963. For people in that generation, that was a defining moment, changing how they saw the world. Its significance prompted their hippocampus not only to capture an image of their surroundings when they heard the news, but to log the emotions and how they connected with and understood the world. In some way, this redefined how they saw the world.

Like it, or not, Brexit (the decision of UK voters in 2016 to leave the European Union) was, to some extent, a defining moment for many British people, bringing a new perspective or way of seeing the world, changing their emotional outlook for good or bad. On an individual level, if you plot key stages of your life by changes – of job, marital status, family, hobbies, friends – you'll be able to identify key defining moments which directed and defined your world. And once you understand what a defining moment is, you can move from merely reacting to such moments to being able to prompt and create them as part of persuading people.

Defining moments *can* be prompted. In the petrified forest in Arizona, there are trees which are now preserved as rock. The process that brought about this change was one where the original spaces and pores in the wood were filled with minerals. The petrified (fossilized rock) trees became replicas of themselves as wood trees (even at a microscopic level). The difference between the two is that what has come into them (the minerals) has enabled their form to remain. A defining moment is like this in so far as it allows a specific action-prompting insight or perspective to enter the mind and cause a specific understanding or view to remain and define a specific area of a person's outlook.

Chapter 14 offers an approach whereby persuasion can act like a bus-sized boulder, influencing a person's outlook and action on a particular issue.

THE GOLDEN RULE OF EMOTIONAL CONNECTION

I remember, towards the end of 2016, receiving a very bold email. It advertised a Webinar, titled 'Why Emotion Will Drive Your Customer Strategy in the Year Ahead'. It claimed:

> In 2017, there will be a new kind of business: a kind that doesn't continue to use the logic of 'touchpoints', 'goals' and 'conversions' but which acts on what really drives people: emotion.

> Emotion is key to delivering far better customer experiences
> . . . Analysts to strategists can start using emotion analysis to
> drive their customer experience strategy in 2017.[6]

It's true. Emotionally connecting is like oxygen, enabling your communication to find its sweet spot – to be 'firebranded' into the Centre Brain and used persuasively.

But there's a golden rule you must hold yourself to:

Show, don't tell.

I love my wife. We met at 21, married at 23, and 18 years on we're in love. Still. One of the reasons is that we show it. My working hours, for example, help to strengthen our emotional connection. I could *tell* her I love her (and I do tell her), but it's what I do on a daily basis that gives her Centre Brain the ability to analyse and reach its own conclusion about my words.

As Kevin Roberts says in his brilliant book *The Lovemarks Effect*, 'Attraction is emotion with purpose.'[7] And the unique thing about emotion is that it must grow from within. It can't be enforced from outside.

The Centre Brain offers deep, lasting engagement and buy-in because it works things out for itself rather than being told. It likes to be shown, not told – so that it can decide to act based on what it's seen (pictures); the ideas it's digested and allowed to generate further ideas; the Why it's understood; and the contrast it's weighed.

This is why all five prompts don't *tell* the Centre Brain anything; instead they offer an input that the Centre Brain can digest for itself. Telling is like giving a GCSE student the answer rather than the question in an exam. The question exists to allow the student to apply and use the learning he or she has. When you do 'tell' or offer the answer rather than the question, you are not persuading people in the way favoured by the action centre: it likes to come to a conclusion on its own. Instead you awaken the Outer Brain and generate a conclusion to what you've tried to tell it – not action.

Let the Centre Brain work out for itself the response by using the prompts outlined in earlier chapters. As it does so, this *becomes* the emotional connection.

CENTRE
BRAIN
COMMUNICATORS

'Good communication is as stimulating as black coffee, and just as hard to sleep after.'
— ANNE MORROW LINDBERGH

'I REMIND MYSELF EVERY MORNING: NOTHING I SAY THIS DAY WILL TEACH ME ANYTHING. SO, IF I'M GOING TO LEARN, I MUST DO IT BY LISTENING.'

– LARRY KING

8   Five great communicators

'Around your mid-twenties your brain's neural pathways begin to solidify. But you can still create new ones.'

If you spend long enough thinking about the following point, it will change your belief in your brain's ability. Regardless of ethnicity or gender, your brain has the same molecular architecture as the brain of the friend, colleague or celebrity you most admire for his or her communication skills and persuasive ability.[1] 'But', you may be thinking, 'my friend/ colleague/favourite celebrity has so much more intelligence or natural ability than I do!' No, what such individuals have is an understanding (intentional or accidentally discovered) of how to prompt their – and their audience's – Centre Brain to respond. You have the same brain architecture, so you can use those same opportunities.

A HIDDEN UNDERGROUND STORE

Apparently (according to a local planning inspector), beneath our back garden, or one of our neighbours' gardens, is a huge old granary store connected to the bakery shop down the road by an ancient passage. It was used in Victorian times to store grain and keep it cool. It has sat there for over a hundred years, untouched.

No one's exactly sure where it is (though planners insist that new foundations must go deeper than usual, just in case).

If we found a way into it, we would probably need to shore up the roof, clear away a century of dust, roof-fall and in-grown roots, and blast some fresh air through. You and I, we have around 100 billion neurons in our brains. Tonight, glance up at the stars. There are around the same number of stars in our galaxy as there are neurons in your brain. And, like that old grain store, some of your neurons are sitting there waiting to be discovered and used. If you're not persuasive in your communication, the problem isn't that you lack potential. The problem may be one of activating the pathways of those neurons.

Around your mid-twenties your brain's neural pathways begin to solidify. But you can still create new ones.[2] The techniques in chapters 10 to 14 are designed to help you do this. When you decide to create new pathways and connections – for example, by turning your message into an idea – you activate a neural pathway you may not normally use. If you're over 25 it's harder work, like opening up a granary store a hundred years after it was closed, rather than just five years. But it's still sitting there, waiting.

This chapter introduces several effective and persuasive communicators, and attempts to identify how the five prompts form a part of their communication. I make no claim that they *intentionally* used the prompts; I'm simply pointing out where they do use them, and showing how the prompts help to make their communication engaging.

You can begin to engage your brain in using the Centre Brain prompts as you read this chapter. For each communicator, I've first framed the piece of communication he or she offers as a challenge. Reflect on the challenge; think about how you would use the prompts to answer it. How might you:

- turn your message into an idea;
- use Why to make What and How interesting;
- introduce contrasting options;
- pictorialize your point;
- create emotional connection?

If answering the challenge proves more complex than you think it should, let it whet your appetite for the simple FireBrand system I have developed, and use, to solve these challenges. You'll discover it when you reach Chapter 9.

Approach each of the communicators with confidence: you can activate the same neural pathways used by any one of them.

JESUS

Around the turn of the century, two millennia ago, a man in the Middle East gave us a masterclass in communicating with the Centre Brain. His name was Jesus. The man Mahatma Gandhi liked. 'I like your Christ,' he said. 'I do not like you Christians. You Christians are so unlike your Christ.'[3]

The task Jesus set himself was mammoth. He announced from the start that he was going to explain a kingdom (the kingdom of God) that is here but somehow *not* here; that is present but also invisible.

A kingdom that despite being often invisible would, he said, change the world. To make matters worse, he was speaking this message to people belonging to a largely Outer Brain civilization. What and How were the foundations; debate and conclusions ruled. There's a pretty convincing analysis in a brilliant wedge of a book, *The Master and His Emissary*, that Western culture is very similar, with its rigid, bureaucratic obsession with structure, its transactional approach to human interaction, and mechanized view of life.[4] Many of us can relate to speaking into such a 'why-shy' culture.

Every time Jesus set out to persuasively communicate, he deployed the five prompts. He turned his message into ideas ('The kingdom of God is *like* . . . a mustard seed').[5] He answered 'why' first. (The story of the woman caught in adultery saw Jesus respond to the question 'What should be done with her?' by explaining why using the law was risky: 'Let any one of you who is without sin be the first to throw a stone at her.')[6]

He used contrast (e.g. rock and sand; sheep and goats; a strong man bound up and weak). He used pictures. (His parable of the Good Samaritan came in answer to the question 'What must I do to inherit eternal life?' and painted a picture which people could use to deduce his answer: be kind, show compassion.)[7]

In a slightly Monty Python-esque encounter, Jesus heals a crippled woman on a holy day and the lawmakers then corner the now healthy woman, telling her that there are six days for working: 'Come and be healed on those days'! Apparently overhearing her account of living crippled for 18 years, they assume an extra 24 hours would have been neither here nor there . . .

Google Luke 13.10–17 and read the short account of Jesus healing the crippled woman on the Sabbath.

CONSIDER THIS CHALLENGE

A sick woman is healed by Jesus on the holy 'Sabbath' day. The lawmakers take issue with the fact that Jesus has healed on a day which is legislated as a day for rest. You have to convince them that the same rules which apparently prevent her healing were meant to be for the benefit of people and animals, and therefore this healing is OK.

How would you do this, using the five prompts?

HOW JESUS TACKLED THIS

Idea

The idea Jesus uses is freedom: why should it be OK for a lawmaker to untie an animal so it can drink freely on the Sabbath, while at the same time banning someone from being freed from suffering on that holy day?

Why

The heart of this issue is hypocrisy. Jesus uses that word. It means the practice of claiming to have higher standards or being more noble or worthy than someone else. Jesus challenges and uproots this idea, so much so that the synagogue leader is left 'humiliated'.

Contrast

Jesus contrasts the releasing of a woman (his action) from what bound her with his critics' action of releasing their livestock from what binds them. In both cases the outcome is good. The contrast helps make clear the foolishness of their rule.

Picture

Jesus uses the donkey to visualize and pictorialize his point.

Emotional connection

The response from the people (they were 'delighted') suggests that an emotional connection had been forged. However, the deeper emotional connection probably came when Jesus called the bent-over woman to approach him, and then healed her.

JOSH SHIPP

Josh was born in 1982 and grew up moving from foster home to foster home. He is now an American youth advocate, youth motivational speaker and bestselling author, and is often referred to as 'The Teen Whisperer'. He began speaking professionally at the age of 17.

CONSIDER THIS CHALLENGE

You're invited to deliver a talk on dealing with hidden challenges. You must approach the subject in a way that makes people willing to accept that they may have inner fears, battles and behaviours that, if not recognized and dealt with, will rear up and ruin their ambitions and plans.

How would you do this, using the five prompts?

HOW JOSH SHIPP TACKLED THIS

Josh delivered a 15-minute talk titled 'What Is Your Tiger?' If you are able, on YouTube enter 'What Is Your Tiger? Josh Shipp' and watch the presentation.

Here's how Josh uses the Centre Brain prompts.

Idea

We all have a metaphorical tiger lurking in us somewhere. While on the loose (or untamed), it's dangerous, and threatens all our ambitions. This is because how we do *anything* is how we do *everything*: it can pounce unexpectedly.

Why

All of us have something in our lives that we have made peace with. But we have no business making peace with our tiger. It will come out of nowhere and destroy our ambitions. We will self-sabotage.

Contrast

Josh introduces the idea of 'self-sabotage' as the contrast between succeeding and sabotaging your success. He talks about the impossibility of keeping personal 'tigers' locked up in certain areas of life; for example, trying to keep them away from business dealings we're involved in.

Picture

A man called Antoine Yates kept a 500-pound tiger in his one-bedroom flat. The police drilled a hole through the door and were shocked to spy the creature. Antoine thought this was completely normal. The animal had grown up with him and he was blind to how dangerous it was.

Emotional connection

Josh Shipp shares vulnerably about his 'tigers'. And he creates an emotional connection to his audience through introducing his own tigers:

I have had a phenomenal year in terms of family and business, and an absolutely terrible year internally. I've made some mistakes and hurt a few people I care about; I had a very good friend betray me and sever a relationship. Then all of these fears, insecurities and doubts come running at me like a 500-pound tiger . . . I am a control freak, so when I get my team involved and get things off my plate, I do a terrible job at it.

BRENÉ BROWN

In 2010 this little-known academic, who worked as an associate professor of social work at the University of Houston, was propelled from relative obscurity into the mainstream as a 'celebrity self-help queen' after giving a TEDx talk on her specialist subject – vulnerability – to several hundred people in Texas.

CONSIDER THIS CHALLENGE

You're invited to communicate the idea that vulnerability, although painful, is also the doorway to creativity, belonging and love.

HOW BRENÉ BROWN TACKLED THIS

Google 'Brené Brown TEDx Houston' and watch the video.

Here's how the Centre Brain prompts form part of Brené Brown's talk.

Idea

Brené Brown draws the many threads into a single idea: what makes you vulnerable is what makes you beautiful. And she offers examples of this: the willingness to say 'I love you' first; the willingness to invest in a relationship that may or may not work out. And she strengthens the idea by showing there's a cost to trying to outsmart it: 'You cannot selectively numb vulnerability. When you numb the bad stuff you also numb the good stuff.'

Why

She creates a baseline which gets to the heart of living: 'Connection is why we're here – the ability to feel connected is why we're here.' This provides the lens through which what she has to say about vulnerability becomes interesting.

Contrast

Brown draws the audience into what could be quite a dry research study by using contrast to explain her interviews in the research phase:

> When you ask people about love, they tell you about heart-break. When you ask people about belonging, they tell you their most excruciating experiences of being excluded. When you ask people about connection, the stories they tell me are about disconnection.

She then introduces the contrast between her preference and the opposite answer she found: 'My mission as a researcher is to control and predict. But I had turned up the answer that the way to live is with vulnerability.'

Picture

Towards the beginning of her talk Brown creates the picture of an ordered rational academic locking horns with an intangible research challenge and attempting to 'deconstruct and outsmart vulnerability'. The picture gains depth and colour as she explains how she framed it to her therapist:

> Here's the thing – I have a vulnerability issue. I know vulnerability is the core of shame and fear and of our struggle for worthiness but it appears it's also the birthplace of joy, creativity, belonging, of love. And I think I have a problem . . .

Emotional connection

Brown generates emotional connection by personalizing what she researched. She makes herself vulnerable in the talk (modelling what she is talking about, although not saying that's what she's doing) by discussing her own crisis point in terms of becoming vulnerable.

PETE GREIG - THE VISION FILM

Inspired by Moravian Christians who started praying in 1727 and carried on, in shifts, for 100 years (google '100 Year Prayer Meeting' for more), Pete Greig, who is something of a modern-day Moravian, opened a prayer room in September 1999: 'I figured that if the Moravians could do a century of 24/7 prayer, we could at least try for a month in our church back home.'

The idea went viral – global even. It found a youth audience and kicked off continuous prayer in many and varied settings, with prayer rooms in the clubs of Ibiza, in churches, even prayer rooms in schools. The movement of non-stop prayer has spread to 100 nations, all praying for nations, people and poverty, with a particular focus on the radical call of faith. Early on, Pete Greig wrote what became known as 'The Vision' in a prayer room at three o'clock one morning.

THE CHALLENGE

How do you motivate a group of young people and young adults to act on the faith they have adopted? To dream, step out and take risks which bring a world into being – a world their faith has promised *can* be created.

How would you do this, using the prompts?

HOW PETE GREIG TACKLED THIS

On YouTube enter 'The Vision Film' and watch the video.

Pete graffitied the vision on the walls of a warehouse prayer room in 1999 as an inspiring and provocative call to action and prayer. It was adopted by millions as 'The Vision' and, in 2016, through crowdfunding, was turned into a film.

In the words of the vision here's how Pete Greig used the Centre Brain prompts.

Idea

'The vision is Jesus – obsessively, dangerously, undeniably Jesus . . . This vision will be. It will come to pass. It will come easily. It will come soon.'

Why

The benefit, or the Why, is projected as a movement of people helping those in need: 'They are free, yet they are slaves of the hurting and dirty and dying . . . the vision is holiness that hurts the eyes – it loves people away from their suicide leaps.'

Contrast

The contrast is between the life people would have lived and the life their faith leads them into:

> They are free from materialism . . . they laugh at 9-to-5 little prisons . . . gave up the game of minimum integrity long ago to reach for the stars . . . scorn the good and strain for the best . . . the army is disciplined . . . young people who beat their bodies into submission. Sacrifice fuels the fire of victory. Can hormones hold them back? Can fear scare them? The advertisers cannot hold them. Hollywood cannot mould them.

Picture

The image is of an army of young people who have accepted and stepped into the radical 'ask' of their faith – and because of it set out to change the world for the better:

> The vision is an army of young people . . . they are free from materialism . . . they could eat caviar on Monday and crusts on Tuesday . . . they are mobile like the wind . . . they belong to the nations . . .

Emotional connection

The emotion is generated in several ways. First, the film embraces the extreme: the Centre Brain is stirred and moved to connect when a contrast is strong – when opposites are presented. The words, ideas, pictures are of a movement of people 'mobile like the wind' yet bound together as 'an army', of 'laying down lives' for the cause. Second, the draw is towards this 'underground' army identity which brings with it an emotional connection of fulfilling faith for the good of the world. Next, the visuals in the film present a powerful sense of momentum, of everyone featured in the film driven towards this unifying vision and of the vision being already brought to life. And finally, the film generates emotion through a sense of coming together for an underground vision, of living in one world while creating another, and of 'the crowds chanting again and again: "Come on"'.

HARRY BAKER - PRIME NUMBERS POEM

Harry Baker has a degree in mathematics and is a brilliant poet. While studying he won the Poetry Slam World Cup, and wrote and performed a five-star sellout Edinburgh Fringe show. He's also an (accidental) international rap battler and his work is published on TED.com.

THE CHALLENGE

How do you make maths, and specifically prime numbers, interesting enough to engage and entertain an audience?

How would you do this, using the prompts?

HOW HARRY BAKER TACKLED THIS

Here's how Harry used the Centre Brain prompts. On YouTube, enter 'Harry Baker: A Love Poem for Lonely Prime Numbers' and watch the video.

Idea

A love story: the idea is of 'odd' prime numbers personified and given personality as 'rough around the edges, yet casually messed'.

The poem tells of the one-sided attraction of a prime number (for the non-prime number, 60, who is 'unimprovable . . . right on time . . . perfectly round') who eventually finds true love.

Why

True love was never about perfect love, but about imperfections finding perfection together.

Contrast

The difference between the perfectly rounded 60 and the contrastingly less 'finished' (yet more engaging) 59 – and 61 – pervades the whole poem:

> Although she lived across the street they came from different worlds.
> While 59 admired 60's perfectly round figure, 60 thought 59 was . . . odd.

Picture

Harry gives simple details of a street in which the numbers 59, 60 and 61 live. The details he gives cause your Centre Brain to create that picture – and enter the story.

Emotional connection

The Centre Brain makes an emotional connection with the idea of not being good enough to attract the person we like: 'She maintained the strict views imposed on her by her mother that separate could not be equal.' In addition, the emotional connection is formed through the story of the underdog, the spurned lover. Rejected by 60, 59 finds deeper happiness:

61 was clever, see, not prone to jealousy.
She looked him in the eyes and told him, quite tenderly:
'You're 59, I'm 61, together we combine
to become twice what 60 could ever be.'

So how do *you* simply and effectively embrace the Centre Brain system? To enable this I developed – and regularly use – a system for applying the prompts to any communication problem . . .

MAKE
IT HAPPEN

'Some people want it to happen.
Some wish it would happen.
Others make it happen.'
— MICHAEL JORDAN

'IN MAKING A SPEECH ONE MUST STUDY THREE POINTS: FIRST, THE MEANS OF PRODUCING PERSUASION; SECOND, THE LANGUAGE; THIRD, THE PROPER ARRANGEMENT OF THE VARIOUS PARTS OF THE SPEECH.'

– ARISTOTLE

9 Your body's ninth system: persuasion

FireBrand: a system for applying the prompts to any communication problem

`Smell, or see, delicious food and your digestive juices activate . . . This is the same as the Centre Brain: when you speak from your Centre Brain . . . you activate [people's] persuasive system.'

As you're reading this, there's more going on throughout your body than you'd think. It's System Central. Up to eight systems are running inside you, each achieving a complex and important task without your having to mastermind the activity.

Picture it as a log-burning stove inside you, always running in the background, providing constant warmth. You feed it at times with fuel, and the heat increases. Staying where there's air (rather than, say, underwater) is your conscious part in enabling your respiratory system to function. Eating food regularly is your conscious part in enabling your digestive system to fuel you. They're subconscious systems, both vital and virtual. And, because they're so automated, they can feel 'unreal'. But you're able to feel their 'warmth' – their beneficial effect.

Your Centre Brain has a system too: the persuasion system.

HARNESSING THE PERSUASION SYSTEM

You've felt the benefits of the persuasion system since birth, whenever you've solved a problem, had an idea, empathized with a friend or made a difficult decision.

And you've fed the persuasion system – by watching things closely and digesting pictures; by asking probing questions and finding out why; by making comparisons to help you make decisions; by wrestling with a message which your Centre Brain absorbs as a feeder for a related idea; by engaging emotionally with people, places and products.

And, just as eating food awakens your digestive system, so the five prompts awaken the persuasive system.

Smell, or see, a delicious food and your digestive juices activate: you feel hunger and yearning for it. A similar thing happens with the Centre Brain: when you speak from your Centre Brain, using the five prompts, you activate the Centre Brain of those you're communicating with – sparking and activating *their* persuasive systems.

Just as a toddler must practise how to use his system – working at using a knife and fork to get food into his mouth – so we must practise using the prompts. The persuasion systems *will* still function if we don't. But by practising, our Centre Brain treads new neural pathways, enabling us to harness and intentionally prompt the persuasive system in those we communicate with.

Knives and forks feature less and less the more remotely you travel. I've eaten a meal of sugar mixed with snow (both delicious and surprisingly energizing), up a mountain half the height of Everest in Bolivia, by pouring the mixture from a small bag into my mouth. I've used my hands to tear and consume a *meshwi* of lamb, slow-cooked for 24 hours on underground coals, in Africa's Sahel region, and have wrestled with chopsticks in Cambodia.

There's a surprising learning curve as you practise eating cleanly using a different system from the knife and fork you grew up with. When you begin to harness the persuasive prompts, it's the same. And, to make this easier, the 'FireBrand system' is a simple framework I have developed and regularly use to help apply the Centre Brain's persuasion prompts to any situation.

It's a system that finds it roots with the Vikings.

THE VIKING BRAND

My ancestors were, apparently, Vikings. My great-grandfather, grand-father and father have all suffered from 'Viking's disease' – medical-ly known as 'Dupuytren's contracture' – brought to Europe and passed down by the Vikings. I've warned my three sons it's coming their way. (If you've noticed an elderly male in your family with contracting hands, don't worry: it's now resolved with a simple operation. My great-grandfather, in the days before the NHS, was not so lucky: he spent his later years unable to hold a knife or fork.)

I've always held the Vikings in some esteem because they were the early inventors of branding. They'd brand cattle, goods and sometimes humans they captured with their specific 'mark' or brand, using an iron, heated in the fire. This 'firebrand' mark was permanent. It left an imprint that stayed.

Today branding has progressed from the notion of a brand as just a physical mark. We now understand that effective branding leaves a much deeper imprint on an audience – in the Centre Brain. This is where you need to 'firebrand' your communication.

THE FIREBRAND SYSTEM

To burn brightly, a fire needs three things:

- a spark
- fuel
- oxygen.

THE SPARK: THE IDEA

I sat with Jim as he lit the fire. He created a spark that ignited some dung, bark and kindling sticks.

The Centre Brain already has the kindling. It just needs the right spark. And the spark is the idea.

The purpose of kindling is to generate enough heat to light the logs of a fire. In the Centre Brain, too, the idea is not an end in itself. Its purpose is to tempt and engage the brain's action centre so that the fire takes hold, grows and firebrands your communication.

THE FUEL: WHY AND CONTRASTING PICTURES

The spark can only progress into a fire with the aid of solid fuel.

The Centre Brain too needs some substance to absorb and bite into in order to generate action. This solid fuel consists of the 'why' and the 'contrasting picture(s)'. They unpack, explain, magnify and grow the idea, without whose spark they'd be logs on the ground without a fire to release the potential inside.

THE OXYGEN: EMOTIONAL CONNECTION

As we sat round the fire that night in rural Africa, a breeze blew through. It grew the fire. We may not always acknowledge the importance of the air around the fire, but shelter the flames too much and the lack of oxygen means the fire can't grow. Fire depends on air – oxygen – just as the Centre Brain depends on emotional connection. It must connect with what's around it. The spark (the idea), and the fuel (the Why and the contrasting picture(s)) depend on the oxygen (emotional connection) to grow the fire and firebrand the communication. As Kevin Roberts, CEO of Saatchi & Saatchi Ideas Company puts it: 'the definition of a great idea . . . it makes a real emotional connection'.[1]

These are the ingredients which come together to firebrand your communication. Below, I unpack how to use the system, using a real-life example.

FIREBRANDING FAIR-TRADE FASHION

My friend Andy runs an 'ethical fashion' label: Visible Clothing. His mission: to make fashion rewarding for the factory worker as well as the buyer. The big problem the company faced was that few in the fair-trade fashion sector were managing to convince the big fashion retailers just how profitable an ethical factory could be. So Andy and his colleagues did what (as far as I can see) few others have done – they bought a factory in India to show them.

Even though this is an important message, its importance doesn't make it vital to an audience. The idea that if you grow good grass (have a worthy message) the sheep will come (people will automatically respond) just isn't borne out in real life. Using the FireBrand system, here's how Andy's message goes from being a message to being an idea which is firebranded into the Centre Brain.

The FireBrand system lets you use the Centre Brain prompts to firebrand your message into the Centre Brain of your audience.

You need three things to make a fire.

1 THE SPARK STARTS IT ALL

- The spark is your idea.
- Use the simple technique in Chapter 10 (page 149) to find your idea.
- Frame this idea around the problem it needs to solve, using the steps below.

The problem

Write a simple description of the problem that the idea will address.

> It's hard work changing the fashion industry when you're on the outside as a purchaser or supplier to the market.

You have little control over the heart of the industry: the factories.

The idea

Present the idea as a response to the problem it's addressing.

> The Trojan Horse
> The Trojan Horse allows you to get through the barriers from outside to inside, to strike at the heart of the problem.

2 THE FUEL GROWS THE FIRE

The fuel is Why (it matters) and a contrasting picture (to visualize the problem).

The Why

Write a line explaining why this idea is important in relation to the problem.

> Fashion-factory workers often get a raw deal (hours, conditions, wages). The alternative is that their children don't eat. But it has proved hard to find an answer to this dilemma.

The contrasting picture which visualizes the idea

> A Trojan Horse (picture) allows you to get through the barriers, freely, from outside to inside (contrast).

3 THE OXYGEN GIVES LIFE TO THE FIRE

The 'oxygen' is emotional connection to your audience: the human face of the problem.

A young mum, Meena, leaves her children in the village, living for six-week periods in a city, working 18-hour shifts in an unsafe fashion-factory, for tiny wages. She suffers but is in no bargaining position: her children must eat.

The FireBrand is the imprint or mark that your communication leaves, using this system (spark, fuel, oxygen). Because it uses the action brain's prompts, it firebrands your communication into the action centre of the brain.

It also provides a structure and form for your communication.

SAMPLE COMMUNICATION

Our Trojan Horse

[The spark: idea]
The Trojan Horse taught us well. We've stopped trying to break a barrier that wouldn't budge.

[The fuel: problem]
Instead, we've climbed *into* the Trojan Horse, gone around the barrier to the inside. Here we can strike the heart of the problem itself, not its barrier.

[The fuel: why]
We're proud of our first two years. We sourced ethical clothing. We showed that ethical fashion doesn't *need* to run at a loss. We helped young mums like Meena, who'd worked 18-hour shifts in terrible conditions for a pittance.

But the costs were high. And our voice often bounced off the high walls protecting the fashion industry. But the Trojan Horse helped us wise up.

[The oxygen: emotional connection]
So, on 12 January this year, we bought a factory. In India. Our Trojan Horse.

As factory owners we're now on the inside, where we're building a model factory which is *also* profitable. Fair wages; good conditions; worker welfare; good returns.

As factory owners with a seat at the table, we'll bring our trade to that table a different way. Profitable *and* fair. A model for what's possible. You were there at the start when we crowdfunded the idea into a small label. You enabled us to build the Trojan Horse, so you were with us in it. We're glad you're still with us. We need you. To make the factory a model of fair fashion. Share our story. Buy the clothes mums like Meena make.

NEURAL PRACTICE MAKES PERSUASIVENESS

Opening up new neural pathways is stretching. But those pathways are waiting to be walked down. If you find it a challenge to use the techniques above, that's good. Because it's your brain utilizing new neural pathways, walking a lesser-used neural track.

I see this repeatedly in my work with organizations to mainstream Centre Brain thinking and make it feel normal – even instinctive: practice does make persuasiveness.

Every time you practise, your brain is making and using new connections, or establishing stronger connections between neurons. According to research at Cornell University, 'The phrase "practice makes perfect" has a neural basis in the brain.'[2] As you repeatedly use new, or widening, neural pathways, it takes your brain less effort each time, and the process becomes more instinctive.

This practice narrows the gap between people often described as 'creatives' and those who see their strengths in a different area. We *all* have similar brain structures. The difference is in how we use them – the neural paths we have trodden and will tread.

As psychologist Mihaly Csikszentmihalyi said (drawing on around 30 years of observing creative people):

> Creative individuals are remarkable for their ability to adapt to almost any situation and to make do with whatever is at hand to reach their goals. If I had to express in one word what makes their personalities different from others, it's *complexity*. They show tendencies of thought and action that in most people are segregated. They contain contradictory extremes; instead of being an 'individual', each of them is a 'multitude'.[3]

I'd argue, based on experience, that this segregation is about practice. Some people will be more naturally 'wired' towards this, but everyone can use the above techniques to begin to awaken or create new neural pathways. They will enable you to host contradictory thoughts, contrasting them to generate brilliant creative ideas. In the 1960s, Dr Frank Barron conducted experiments with some of the high-level creatives of his day. He observed that 'complexity, at its best, makes for originality and creativeness, a greater tolerance for unusual ideas'.[4]

The techniques that follow, if practised, will help your brain to embrace contradiction and begin to generate ideas.

'IDEAS ARE LIKE RABBITS. YOU GET A COUPLE AND LEARN HOW TO HANDLE THEM AND PRETTY SOON YOU HAVE DOZENS.'

– JOHN STEINBECK

10 A technique for finding ideas

Simple approaches to extract your idea from your message

'An idea always answers a problem or failure. This is why ideas are so transformative for prompting action.'

Whenever you communicate with someone, his or her Centre Brain is looking for concepts, or ideas, within what you say or show. Mary Potter, a professor of brain and cognitive sciences at MIT, says of recent research which shows the brain reading images in 13 milliseconds: 'The fact that you can do that at these high speeds indicates to us that what vision does is find concepts.'[1] A concept is an idea in a more workable, applied form – more ready for the audience. And an idea is a message that's been reworked for the Centre Brain.

HIT THE GROUND RUNNING (DON'T JUST HIT THE GROUND)

Ideas are the Centre Brain's mother tongue. In the FireBrand model they're the spark that starts the furnace. So we must speak to the Centre Brain in order to persuade others.

A sobering note: advertising agencies charge high fees when organizations ask for the 'idea' that will change everything for them. And ideas can – and do – enable that change. Before the idea of soap and handwashing, deaths among children under the age of five were even higher than they are today. Henry Ford had the idea of the car. There's little evidence he actually made the following comment, though it's often attributed to him online: 'If I had asked people what they wanted, they would have said "Faster horses".' But whether those were his words or not, his achievements suggest he knew that ideas step outside the current neural pathways, or ways of seeing the world, and forge new ones by bringing together things not previously connected. Don't therefore expect to 'nail it' immediately. But do expect to nail it. Remember, it's practice that makes persuasiveness.

This chapter includes two techniques for extracting an idea from your message: 'Opposites Appeal' and 'Random Connections'.

IDEAS TECHNIQUE 1: OPPOSITES APPEAL

I developed this idea and use it with individuals and organizations, helping them turn their message into an idea (and their idea into a basic concept). I refer to it as the 'Opposites Appeal' approach because it enables you to use 'opposites' to generate a strong idea, which makes your message appealing.

START WITH WHAT YOU KNOW: WRITE DOWN YOUR
MESSAGE FROM THE COMMUNICATOR'S POINT OF VIEW

Be as specific as you can when framing the message you want to communicate and persuade people towards – as if you were verbalizing it as an invite or offer to a person:

We'd like you to come to our new youth club in the centre of town, Friday nights.

WRITE DOWN WHAT FAILURE WOULD LOOK LIKE FOR THIS MESSAGE FROM THE COMMUNICATOR'S POINT OF VIEW

An idea always answers a problem or failure. This is why ideas are so transformative for prompting action – they speak to, and begin to answer, these problems and the failure they lead to. The problems lie at the root of your audience's fear (which, in turn, is what prevents engagement).

The youth club is boring and we're not sure anyone else will come.

This looks like an empty club that would embarrass anyone who did come in.

WRITE DOWN THE *OPPOSITE* OF THAT PROBLEM/FEAR AND WHAT IT MEANS

It is vital to force your brain to enter territory which, when you're facing what feels like an uphill struggle, seems alien. Whatever the Centre Brain pictures, it begins to act towards. Normally, in situations of anxiety ('No one will come!') your Centre Brain will respond with a picture of what that looks like (an empty youth club). This may prompt action in the form of a negative thought: 'Let's drop the idea.' It's therefore essential to force yourself to picture what success and its consequences look like.

The opposite of no one coming is that too many come. This means that only the first 50 would get in.

EXTRACT YOUR IDEA FROM THE 'OPPOSITE OF THE PROBLEM' ANSWER ABOVE

What you've written above reveals your audience's 'why'. And your idea answers that Why: 'Why must I, as a young person, get there and be part of this club?' Capture this in very basic form – in three to five words.

> Demand is high.

WRITE DOWN A PERSONAL APPLICATION OF THE IDEA, APPLIED TO AN INDIVIDUAL

This helps you to 'flesh out' your idea and turn it into a concept (the idea in a more workable, applied form). Do this by selecting one of the benefits of your offer to the target individual and presenting it through the lens of the message and the idea.

Benefit + Message + Idea = Concept

> Benefit: table football
>
> +
>
> Message: We'd like you to come to our new youth club in the centre of town, Friday nights
>
> +
>
> Idea: Demand is high
>
> =
>
> Concept

- Target the concept at an individual, not a generic group.
- Think about what the individual's actual engagement will look like.
- This concept can be used in your promotion.

Our table footy has eight handles. Want to get your hands on one and be in the game? Demand is high. Latecomers, join the queue!

IDEAS TECHNIQUE 2: RANDOM CONNECTIONS

Another technique I use draws on the brain's love of contrast and comparison, and will help your brain generate new ideas which will prompt the brain to respond. It's as old as the hills. I didn't invent it, but have framed it in the way I often use it.

The technique has a strong track record:

- Einstein used it to understand paradox: he imagined an object in motion and at rest at the same time. This led him to discover the theory of relativity.
- Picasso used it to achieve his cubist perspective: he mentally tore objects apart and then rearranged the elements, presenting them from a dozen points of view simultaneously.
- Alexander Graham Bell invented the telephone using this approach: he reflected on the contrast between the bones in the human ear and their relative size compared to the delicate thin membranes which operated them. His idea came when he applied this contrast of 'delicate moving massive' and wondered whether a membrane could move steel as if it were the bones of the ear. The idea of the telephone was conceived.
- Steve Jobs (and colleagues) used it to bring together a computer and a phone and create the smartphone.

The idea here is simple. You contrast your communication challenge (your message) with an object around you – literally any object – and use the insight into that object's usage to provide the idea for your communication challenge.

As you read now, imagine a cat with two heads. Now envisage your mother as a young child. And a goldfish with arms. Think of a beach – on the red planet, Mars. At a simple level, this is your brain bringing together opposites. In your head is a massive ability to create new pictures – and ideas – by bringing together opposites.

There are many and varied ways you can apply this technique. Below is the approach I take.

START WITH WHAT YOU KNOW: WRITE DOWN THE MESSAGE YOU NEED AN IDEA FOR

> My boss is leaving. I'm ready to step into his job and hold the role until it's advertised (and I apply). I need to convince my boss's boss that I'm up to stepping into it in the interim.

LOOK AROUND AND PICK *ANY* RANDOM OBJECTS: WRITE DOWN EACH OBJECT'S SPECIFIC BENEFIT

Tissue

> Benefit: small and fragile yet makes a massive impact if you have a cold.

Candle

> Benefit: negligible in daylight. After dark, the candle changes the whole perspective of a room and allows

the most basic functions to continue (you can't play a game in the dark).

Dressing gown

Benefit: an extra layer to quickly add or remove when the cold hits and you're not warm enough to cope with it (when you've just climbed out of bed).

Smartphone

Benefit: makes your solitary moments feel connected. Provides eyes to the world even when you're not physically there.

Light switch

Benefit: lights a whole space in one simple flick because of the power (electricity) that it carries and releases. Changes your whole view of what's before you.

USING THE SPECIFIC BENEFIT YOU'VE IDENTIFIED FOR EACH OF THESE OBJECTS, WRITE DOWN, FOR EACH OBJECT, WHAT THE RELATED GENERIC IDEA IS

The generic idea for each item is already *within* the benefit, existing in a specific relationship to the item. This step is about extracting the idea from the specific item and presenting it in a generic way. For example, if the item is a bottle, the benefit is that it allows you to carry something normally hard to transport by hand (e.g. liquid) in a leak-proof way, and it's shaped in a form you can drink from. Then the generic idea is that the bottle makes something easy which would otherwise be difficult. Find this generic idea for each of the benefits you identified.

Tissue

- Benefit: small and fragile yet makes a massive impact if you have a cold.
- Generic idea: a small thing can have a massive impact – enabling an important change.

Candle

- Benefit: negligible in daylight. After dark, the candle changes the whole perspective of a room and allows the most basic functions to continue.
- Generic idea: at the right moment, a small change can transform everything.

Dressing gown

- Benefit: an extra layer to quickly add or remove when the cold hits and you're not ready for it.
- Generic idea: fast impact – right when it's needed.

Smartphone

- Benefit: makes your solitary moments feel connected. Provides eyes to the world even when you're not physically there.
- Generic idea: feeling connected when you're absent is possible. Don't let distance stop you.

Light switch

- Benefit: lights a whole space in one simple flick because of the power (electricity) that it carries and releases. Changes your whole view of what's before you.

- Generic idea: the smallest flicks can have the biggest impact – releasing the waiting power to fulfil their purpose.

WITH YOUR ORIGINAL MESSAGE IN MIND, WRITE DOWN HOW ANY OF THE GENERIC IDEAS COULD BE USED TO CONVEY THIS MESSAGE IN IDEA FORM

[Original message]

My boss is leaving. I'm ready to step into his job and hold the role until it's advertised (and I apply). I need to convince my boss's boss that I'm up to stepping into it.

Tissue

- Generic idea: when you don't have a cold, a tissue is unnecessary. When a cold comes with a continual runny nose, a tissue is a life-saver. The situation changes the impact a tissue has.
- Situational application: you don't always know the impact someone will have until the opportunity arises for them to show it. I'd like to use this vacancy gap as an opportunity to demonstrate how I can have a positive impact in our success as a team.

Light switch

- Generic idea: smallest flicks can have the biggest impact, releasing the power waiting to fulfil its purpose.
- Situational application: if you invite me to step into this role, in the vacancy gap, I'm confident you'll like the impact I'm able to make because it will release

and put to work so much waiting ambition for the organization.

I normally select the best two generic ideas to use. The indicators that they are the best include the criteria listed here.

1   There's a natural connection between the generic ideas and your message.
2   The idea is generative. This means it prompts further thinking, even ideas. In short, it interests and engages you.
3   The idea equals and slightly exceeds the power of any competing ideas coming from others who also seek to persuade.

'ONCE YOU KNOW THE "WHY"
YOU BECOME THE SECOND
MOUSE. YOU UNDERSTAND.
YOU GET THE CHEESE.'
                    – STEVE ADAMS

11 A technique for finding the Why

A simple approach to extract the Why

'One indication you're speaking to the Centre Brain is when people in your audience ask "why" questions first.'

When writers, speakers – any communicators – are not clear on their 'why', they bore people. And boredom has its giveaways. In the 1800s a very wise man decided to measure 'fidget'. His name was Sir Francis Galton and his findings were published in an 1885 paper, 'The Measurement of Fidget'.

When our Centre Brains are not stimulated, we fidget. I was working overseas several years ago, and on my last evening in the country was invited to a farewell meal, after which those around the table had five minutes each to offer a reflection on the work we'd done.

Most kept to the allotted time, give or take a few minutes. But then the head of the project arose. After 25 minutes, he'd finished describing events surrounding the evening he first got the phone call suggesting I visit. People began to fidget. Visibly. One fellow made an excuse and left. Another fell fast asleep. As I watched the others, their fidgeting reflected an inner frustration – almost as if their Centre Brain was saying, 'If what you're saying won't prompt any response, or engagement, I'll generate my own action and movement.' Intriguingly, alongside some fidgeting, I felt like laughing. As we reached the hour mark, I was having to bury my face in my hands to stop involuntary chuckles escaping: my brain's way of seeking an exit?

Sir Francis Galton's research found that people who are bored slouch more. So, he suggested, when you're communicating well with the members of an audience (which means, speaking to their Centre Brains) they should be upright and still. If they begin to slip down their seats and fidget, he concluded, you're probably losing them; in my terms, you're speaking to their Outer Brains.

Sir Francis Galton described a long-winded presentation by a British explorer as he illustrated the geography of explored Africa. Galton refers to the fidgeting of a man in the audience, John Hanning Speke, as the presentation went on. It's worth noting that Speke was himself an explorer: a memorial stands in Kensington Gardens, London, honouring his discovery of Lake Victoria. The presentation should have engaged him. But it didn't. Speaking on a subject supposedly of interest to your audience isn't enough, unless you use the right prompts.

> As he listened to Murchison unfurl the Union Jack in one
> far corner of the globe after another, Speke began to fidget,

exclaiming half loud, 'Oh, I cannot stand this any longer.' He got up to go out. The man nearest to him said, 'Shall you want your chair again, sir? May I have it? Shall you come back?' And he answered, 'I hope not', and left the hall.[1]

Leaving the meeting prematurely proved fatal for Speke. He died later that night, accidentally shooting himself while climbing over a hedge.

THE BRAIN'S 'TEMPLATE' PROTECTION

To bore, or to be bored, is needless – and, as Speke's story suggests, not without consequence. But how do you know when you're boring someone? Knowing your own brain's 'bored signals' helps you spot when your own communication is boring.

In a boring conversation, your Outer Brain deploys its 'templates' (see page 36) to manage being bored by someone. My template answers (which attempt to sound engaged, but reveal boredom) include 'Oh wow!', 'That's really interesting' and 'That's so funny' (though the absence of laughter is the giveaway). At those moments, because I'm operating from the Outer Brain template mode, I also revert to very simple Outer Brain 'what' and 'how' questions: 'Oh, that's really interesting. What's the next step?' This is because my Centre Brain (and it's deeper, more engaged 'why' questions) is not being awoken or activated by the speaker's communication. When it's not a conversation but a presentation, your Centre Brain prompts fidgeting.

The next time you're bored by someone, if it's a conversation, note the templates your Outer Brain deploys to manage this. And begin to notice when those you're communicating with are deploying similar templates in response to you. If it's a presentation, not a conversation, look also for fidgeting.

One indication you're speaking to the Centre Brain is when people in your audience ask 'why' questions first; their eyes watch you (rather than the floor or the room); they jump in with questions at the first opportunity (or even interrupt). Or, if it's a presentation, they sit attentive, still and engaged.

I developed, and use, the technique below to help you work out how to start with Why.

WHAT'S YOUR WHY?

THE WHAT AND HOW

Write down the What and How of the thing you want to communicate. This will normally be discovered by asking yourself what information you want to communicate.

> I'm organizing a hiking trip to the Lakes for friends from an old sports team. It's in July next year, will be for five days and will cost £250. And I want members of the old team to come!

THE GENERAL WHY

Ensure your Why is a response to the What by using what you wrote above as the focus and writing down the reasons why you want to persuade people to get involved: what is your motivation for communicating this?

We had such unity as a team and went through many good experiences together. Those friendships are too good to be lost – and getting together would be refreshing, invigorating, and provide a fresh perspective by drawing on memories of life back then.

THE SPECIFIC WHY BENEFIT

Draw out of the above general Why answer the point that represents the strongest benefit to the audience. Make it personal. This is your Why.

Let's draw on memories of back then to inspire us now.

THE WHAT AND HOW THROUGH THE WHY LENS

As Chapter 4 explains, your What or How should never lead persuasive communication, but needs to be presented through the lens of the Why. Use your above Why and write down, in a personal way, the What and How message seen through that lens.

Why

Let's get together for a few days, reminisce and laugh about our victories – and defeats – 20 years ago, and be inspired by what we achieved – even freshen up our current outlook through this.

What and How

If that's what you need, and you can make it sometime in July next year, for five days' walking in the Lakes (for a snip of a price at £250), then just hit 'reply'.

'CONTRAST HELPED YOU OUT
OF BED THIS MORNING.'
                    – STEVE ADAMS

12 A technique for using contrast

A simple approach to help you work out how to use contrast

'Anything that has a purpose or benefit will have an opposite.'

In Chapter 5 I introduced the 'brain scales'. Imagine your audience's brain scales, on to both ends of which you must place something if you want a decision to be made: each person's brain will weigh both ends against each other to make a decision. And, if the other four prompts frame what's on both ends, you will persuade your listener.

I was presenting and applying Centre Brain communication to staff members at a charity in the south of England. Their offices are in a beautiful house set in large grounds. The room were in overlooked a lake with an attractive old stone bridge crossing it.

We were covering 'contrast', looking at how to use contrast as a tool in communicating. I was suggesting to my listeners that many objects around them have contrast potential which can be harnessed to present an idea:

> A chair introduces the contrast between standing and sitting. If you were communicating to the team you manage, talking about the importance of staying ready and active, you might use the chair to capture the contrast and give the Centre Brain a way to visualize the two ends of the scales.

> A coat represents the contrast between being cold or warm. You could use this if you were debating with your partner whether to get contents insurance. He or she thinks you have yet to own much of value, and since you're living in a fourth-floor flat, a break-in is unlikely. But you'd like to know that your stuff is covered. You ask your partner to stand outside with a coat on (let's assume it's winter). And then take it off. You use the idea of having something surrounding you to convey the benefits of insurance – stopping you from having to focus on the 'cold' (or the worry of 'what if . . .').

Everything has an opposite. A cup of water says something about the contrast between being thirsty and hydrated. A pair of glasses represents the contrast between seeing clearly and having blurred vision. All objects offer ways to visualize a point, and its contrast, for the Centre Brain.

We were discussing one of the training courses the charity ran: 'Effective People Leadership', and how the members of staff could advertise it in a way that spoke directly to the Centre Brain, and thus prompt people to respond and consider signing up.

I spotted the old bridge through the window, and suggested that they imagine if, instead of a description of the 'what' and 'how' in their promotional communication leaflet, they made a short film. In the film, the course leader would stand on one side of the bridge and introduce the course by saying:

> In any group you lead, there'll be some people who will feel they haven't got much to offer. Some even want to get into the water and go under - to hide. Let's imagine they're on one side of the bridge.

As the camera rolls, the course leader would then walk across the bridge, and say:

> In the same group but at the opposite end of the spectrum, you'll find people who seem to be ready to walk on the water, do the impossible, dream big dreams. The commonality is destination: as leader you need them all to be moving towards the same destination. And to work together well they need a leader. Leadership isn't 'one size fits all'. This course gives you strategies, insights and ideas for how to get everyone over the bridge, on to the same side.

The film would then cut to the course leader, who has crossed to the other side of the bridge and concludes the film by saying:

> Rather than having one or two of the team on the oppo-
> site bank, as observers, we'll help you to master effective
> people leadership. Sign up now.

Contrast pinpoints the choice that the Centre Brain is persuaded by. Look around you now, pick any object and ask yourself what is the benefit gained from using this object, and the consequence of not using it. Even the most abstract items have contrast: a brick in a wall offers the benefit of supporting the roof. Without that brick, and others near it, the roof would drop. With it, you remain dry and secure.

CONTRAST PERSUASION

This simple 'contrast persuasion' technique can help you identify contrast within the point you are making.

WRITE DOWN THE POINT YOU WANT TO MAKE AND PERSUADE PEOPLE TO RESPOND TO

> We need to take a new product to market, in an already
> busy marketplace. It's an app that tells you and your
> friendship group, family, children (whoever) where you
> all are at any time.

IDENTIFY THE BENEFIT THIS OFFERS, AND THE COST OF *NOT* USING IT

Anything that has a purpose or benefit will have an opposite, or contrast. If you can't work out the benefit, it's unlikely you'll persuade anyone else to embrace the idea or product.

> Connection versus isolation.

WRITE DOWN A SCENARIO OR SITUATION IN WHICH THIS BENEFIT (OR COST) BECOMES IMPORTANT TO YOUR AUDIENCE

> My daughter is at a party with friends. I want to know she's staying in that place and, when her group walks back, to know they're not taking any detours.

Or:

> I'm starting a new business and am thinking of employing a salesperson to visit clients. It would help me to know the progress he's making as he travels to clients, without my having to be in constant contact.

Use this framing of the contrast as a part of how you persuade your audience.

'IMAGES STRIKE QUICKLY
AND STRIKE HARD, CUTTING
THROUGH LANGUAGE TO
SPEAK DIRECTLY WITH
OUR EMOTIONS, OUR
IMAGINATIONS; HOW WE
KNOW REALITY.'

– TOM PRICE,
PHOTOGRAPHER

13 A technique for extracting the picture

A simple approach to pictorializing your point

'Every picture needs to be connected to the world your listeners live in. The larger the gap . . . the lower the chance they'll respond.'

When I was aged 18 and learned French in Belgium (you may be able to recall my tale of incessant door-knocking in the first chapter), I discovered that the right-sounding word can in fact create the wrong sort of connection, which, of course, isn't particularly helpful when you want to communicate effectively.

One of my language helpers was a girl of 18 who would give me an hour a week to learn a new set of words. We were learning about items in a bedroom. She'd point to an object and say the word within a sentence. She pointed at a wall in her room absolutely plastered in posters. '*J'ai de nombreuses affiches sur mon mur*' (I have many posters on my wall), she said. I meant to reply, '*Oui! Tu as beaucoup*' (Yes, you have many). What I hadn't learned was that while *beaucoup* means 'many' or 'much' in French, to my novice ear a very slight adjustment in how the word is pronounced makes it sound like *beau cul* – or nice bum! I told the 18-year-old: Yes, you have a nice bum!

THE PERSUASION GAP

There's always a gap between what I say and my listener's reality. In that moment, what I said made no sense in the Belgian girl's reality (though she immediately laughed and understood my pronunciation mistake). If you can bridge the gap, you can persuade. If you fail to, even using the language your brain sees in – pictures – won't help you.

There's a fine line between whether a powerful, awe-inspiring story paints a picture which inspires engagement and belief among listeners that they can achieve a similar outcome, or whether it creates distance.

Every picture needs to be connected to the world your listeners live in. The larger the gap between the picture and its related story, and *their* world, the lower the chance they'll respond to the story with action.

While writing this book I was listening to a motivational speaker trying to inspire people using stories of others who had succeeded through giving everything, going the whole distance. The problem was that she didn't bridge the gap between the stories (and the people in the stories) and what her audience did. And not bridging this gap meant she allowed the stories to create a gap between the hearers and the outcome she wanted from her communication. In speaking to an audience member afterwards, it emerged that the person idolized a character in one of the stories, but clearly felt inadequate to ever do anything comparable: the persuasion gap had been created.

If you can show the Centre Brain, in pictorial form, how that gap is crossed, from what is not yet – but could be – to a better result, you can mobilize all the persuasive power in your story.

PICTURES THAT PROMPT THE CENTRE BRAIN

Pictures that speak to your Centre Brain, and have power to persuade, normally have three aspects:

1 They include one or more living things (people or animals), not just locations or items.
2 They create emotional connection between you and the person/animal.
3 They have a scenario or event unfolding in them: they're not static. (Note: A picture that is static, e.g. 'girl sits on ground, bird sits nearby', will need to be turned into a scenario. For example, 'starving little girl sits in the dust, watched by a vulture' (google 'Kevin Carter vulture and girl images'). This is how a scenario adds narrative and emotion to the picture.)

A simple technique to generate a picture which does this is outlined below.

START BY WRITING DOWN THE POINT OR MESSAGE THAT YOUR PICTURE WILL AMPLIFY

Use a person, a group of people or an animal as your focus. The example I use below is from a school-exclusion charity I worked with (all examples are based on fabricated individuals):

Many teenagers are at risk of being excluded from their school. And a small input can make the vital difference. We need you to donate to our charity and sponsor a coach who will talk to, support and enable an at-risk young person: helping that teenager to become the person that he or she could be.

THINK ABOUT A TYPICAL SCENARIO OR ACTIVITY INVOLVING THE SITUATION/PERSON YOU COVER IN YOUR POINT (ABOVE)

It's helpful to bullet-point this scenario.

- Caroline is 14.
- She struggled to make friends when she moved north.
- To win friends she misbehaved.
- Seeing that this won her attention, she pushed her behaviour even more to the extremes.
- She's now at the point of exclusion from school.
- A coach began to meet Caroline. She helped her to unearth her frustration and consider the consequences of her behaviour, and coached her in how to build friendships without misbehaving.

IDENTIFY WHERE IN THE STORY THE EMOTIONAL CONNECTOR IS

You do this by asking yourself which aspect of the scenario evokes any empathy, pity or emotional concern in you. This is where the emotional connection occurs.

Caroline struggled to make friends. [This is the emotional connector.]

STARTING WITH THAT EMOTIONAL CONNECTOR, WRITE THE STORY DOWN OR TELL IT (OUT LOUD)

Use the framework set out here.

The emotional connector

Caroline, aged 14, moved 300 miles from home. She struggled to make new friends. She felt alone.

The jeopardy or problem this emotional connector led to

The only way Caroline's peers took notice of her was when she began disobeying the teacher. She liked feeling connected, so misbehaved more. It got so bad she faced being excluded.

The solution or opportunity which you want to persuade your audience to act on

One of our school coaches began to meet Caroline. She helped her to unearth her frustration and consider the consequences of her behaviour, and coached her in how to build friendships without misbehaving. Caroline rose to the challenge and, six months on, has two good friendships and is no longer at risk of exclusion.

Once you've identified the emotional connector, you have 'oxygen' that allows you to trigger persuasion, using the prompts. As actor Hugh Jackman said: 'We all have triggers to any stage of emotion. It's not always easy to find but it's still there.'[1]

'WE'RE ACTUALLY INFECTED
BY THE EMOTIONS OF
OTHERS.'

– MARCO TAMIETTO,
NEUROSCIENCE RESEARCHER

14 A technique for generating emotional connection

A simple approach to finding the emotional hooks

'When you communicate to persuade, the Centre Brain of your audience is reaching out, attempting to connect emotionally by imitating.'

Emotionally connecting is like oxygen to a fire, enabling your communication to find its sweet spot – to be 'firebranded' into the Centre Brain.

But hold close to the golden rule of emotional connection outlined at the end of Chapter 7:

Show, don't tell.

Remember that the Centre Brain offers deep, lasting engagement and buy-in because it works things out for itself rather than being told. It likes to be shown, not told – so that it can decide to act based on what it's seen (pictures); the idea it's digested and allowed to generate further ideas; the Why it's understood; and the contrast it's weighed.

Below is an example of why allowing emotional connection to grow is so important.

When I work on Centre Brain with charities, churches and other organizations, I sometimes tell the story (and show the TV ad) of a large and well-known UK charity which contracted a successful director to make a Direct-Response TV (DRTV) advert for its cause. A young, soon to become well-known female actor starred in it. And yet when the advert was shown on non-terrestrial channels, it generated (a reliable source suggested) a grand total of four responses. The missing ingredient? Emotional connection.

A FLAME WITHOUT OXYGEN

The advert ticked all the boxes. Using the FireBrand system, it had the spark of an idea (the actor portrayed a girl who'd spent years in care, consumed by pain and guilt); it had the fuel which should have ignited (it offered contrast – to seek help, or not?). It answered the Why (because if the girl summons the strength to get in touch with the charity we, the viewers, must allow the charity to be there to receive her). It painted a picture (a young girl, tears on her face, fighting to take the step and seek help).

Yet the spark was like a flame with a glass placed over it: it lacked the oxygen which emotional connection brings. There wasn't enough emotional connection to allow the Centre Brain to be 'infected' by the emotion. It was a static picture being painted.

When you communicate to persuade, the Centre Brain of your audience is reaching out, attempting to connect emotionally by imitating.

Your brain needs connection. Whether you're a thinker or a feeler (there is estimated to be about a 50/50 split between these two types of people in any given population) has nothing to do with your need for emotional connection. Without it, the emotions won't simply close down, they'll prompt a person to disengage – as viewers of that advert did.

'Men in our society have been conditioned to believe that connecting to emotions is a sign of weakness', wrote Raphael Cushnir in *Psychology Today*. 'Yet this is a losing strategy, because wherever emotions are disparaged or denied, they run the show even more forcefully from behind the scenes.'[1]

So how can you ensure you turn the tap on fully?

HOW DO YOU BRING ABOUT EMOTIONAL CONNECTION?

When my wife Ruth gave birth to our first child, Aidan, she was in hospital, connected to the oxygen system. The oxygen was free-flowing, fast and plentiful. And it seemed to me (as an emotionally connected observer) to be hitting exactly the right spot. For our second baby we had a home birth and the oxygen came from a cylinder brought by the midwife. It was a lot less effective. Less oxygen seemed to reach Ruth (or me, when I tested it!) and it didn't have the same impact.

The strength of the emotional connection you create will determine the response you generate. In oxygen terms, a slower or weaker connection will still prompt the Centre Brain, but will limit the persuasive power. An unlimited supply, however, will enable a defining moment (see Chapter 7, page 97) which not only persuades but also alters – even redefines – your whole view, and response.

The phrase 'emotional contagion' is used to describe what happens when mirror neurons enable emotion to be triggered from (or apparently even to travel from) one person, who *feels* an emotion, to another who *receives* and mirrors it. Crying while watching a film, or feeling some other emotion on account of events in the film, occurs because the emotion in the film is contagious through your mirror neurons, which perceive it and reflect it in you.

So emotional connection must begin with an emotion being displayed or experienced – which can then be copied.

But how can you bring about that emotional connection? Here's a technique I use, which employs the FireBrand system discussed in Chapter 9. I introduce the technique by summarizing it, and then applying it through a short film. If you're able to, watch the film online now, before reading on.

So google and watch: 'Thousands Learn the Hard Way, Prince's Trust'. And refresh yourself on the FireBrand system on pages 140–5.

WORK OUT, AND WRITE DOWN, THE SPARK (IDEA)

You may want to use one of the techniques in Chapter 10 (page 150) to help you identify the idea. In the film this was:

> Even in hardship, inner strength and skill can prevail.

WORK OUT, AND WRITE DOWN, WHAT THE FUEL IS
The Why that answers why the idea matters

Use the technique in Chapter 11 (page 164) to help you identify your Why.

In the film the 'why' of the idea is that hardship doesn't end potential – it grows it, if we help people to realize it.

The contrast which captures the choice between acting on and not acting on the idea

Use the technique in Chapter 12 (page 170) to help you identify your contrast.

In the film this was expressed by using situations that have contrasting endings – and the skill and strength of the young people gets them through.

The picture which represents the idea in visual form

Use the technique in Chapter 13 (page 175) to help you identify your picture.

In the film this was pictured through young people facing tough situations, and pulling through, because they use their inner strength and skill.

WRITE DOWN WHICH EMOTIONS ARE GENERATED OR CAN BE FELT FROM WHAT YOU'VE WRITTEN ABOVE

You may want to consult this (non-exhaustive) list of emotions to stimulate thinking:

- Love
- Trust
- Doubt
- Fear
- Courage
- Surprise
- Friendship/loyalty
- Shame
- Disgust
- Anger
- Sadness
- Anticipation/expectation
- Joy
- Kindness
- Envy
- Pity
- Hope

This is the 'oxygen' or emotional connection.

In the film the emotional connection is created when you see a young person, in an obviously tough situation, showing strength and a determined spirit. Because this is presented using the prompts, the Centre Brain is engaged and you desire to step in.

In the film, this idea is translated into the end screen:

> Thousands of young people learn the hard way.

It then flows directly into the invite. Ensure your invite, or the 'ask' you are seeking to persuade on, is a direct follow-through from what your audience has been moved by. In the film, the emotional connection flows directly into the invite:

> We can help them realize their potential.

'YOU MAY DELAY, BUT
TIME WILL NOT.'
		— BENJAMIN FRANKLIN

15 What you put in = what you get out

A better way of prompting action in people

'By changing the way you use communication, you can use your communication to inspire change.'

My friend Steph had a very frightening couple of hours one evening last August. She and her husband had been at a garden party which ran late into the summer night. At the party a friend told her about a situation in her own family, which absorbed Steph's thoughts and led to what happened when she got home.

Being a Type 1 diabetic, Steph injects two types of insulin each day. The first is known as 'fast-acting'. Whenever Steph eats, she injects a small amount. Around six units are enough to absorb all the glucose in a medium-sized meal. The insulin acts quickly and is powerful.

The second type of insulin is known as 'long-acting'. It's absorbed slowly, over a 24-hour period. Steph injects a lot more of this type – 32 units – each evening.

Fast-acting insulin is powerful stuff. In 2015 a medical mystery of unexplained deaths in a UK hospital was solved with the conviction of a nurse who had killed two patients using insulin. Insulin enables the glucose in food to be absorbed. But too much of it literally absorbs *all* the body's sugar reserves.

Steph tells it like this:

> We arrived home late, tired and thinking on what my friend had told me. I wasn't concentrating, hadn't put the light on and, fumbling around in the fridge for the long-acting insulin, I drew up the normal 32 units, but of the wrong insulin. I injected 32 units of the fast-acting type. As I withdrew the syringe, I stared in horror at it, realizing what I'd done.

Around seven units of fast-acting insulin would, for Steph, be enough to absorb the sugar in a good-sized meal. So 32 units of this type was enough to gobble up every last gramme of sugar in her body.

She knew she was now in a race.

> I sat down to keep my heart rate slow, as insulin absorbs faster when your pulse rises. I knew the act of calling an ambulance would take several minutes – minutes in which the insulin would start kicking in.

Instead Steph called her husband, who went straight for the honey. While Steph spooned it into her mouth, he dissolved sugar into warm water, poured orange juice and peeled a banana.

The race was between Steph's digestive system and the insulin. Could her body release the glucose from the food and drink faster than the insulin could absorb it?

Every time you communicate, a race is happening: will the Centre Brain be prompted before the Outer Brain can deploy a template to close off any response?

When communication happens, two different forces are always at play; one leads to conclusions, the other to action. And the one you prompt will be the one that responds.

Steph ate for an hour, non-stop, that night, and because of the quick thinking of her husband with the honey, she was fine.

The five prompts to generate response in the people you communicate with can change everything. Or nothing. They can help forge the tomorrow you imagine, if you use them.

Augustine of Hippo put it like this: 'God has promised forgiveness to your repentance, but he has not promised tomorrow to your procrastination.'[1] At the start of this book, I made you a promise of my own: this book won't offer you a one-size-fits-all magic button to press whenever you need to inspire people to action. Instead, by giving you an understanding of the Centre Brain and its various prompts, it will enable you to *create* the 'magic button' suited to the situation, whenever you need to inspire people.

By changing the way you use communication, you can use your communication to inspire change.

Now, what you do with that is up to you . . .

Notes

2 THE POINT IS TO UNDERSTAND

1 From a booklet produced in 1991 by Burnett Works – Leo Burnett's London-based fundraising and marketing agency – containing 100 quotes by Leo Burnett, to celebrate the hundredth anniversary of his birth in 1891.

2 Edward R. Murrow, speaking as Director of the United States Information Agency (USIA), in testimony before a congressional committee, Washington DC, May 1963.

3 Salman Rushdie, in '1,000 Days Trapped inside a Metaphor', an address given at Columbia University, New York, 12 December 1991.

4 Scott Barry Kaufman and Carolyn Gregoire, *Wired to Create: Unravelling the mysteries of the creative mind* (New York: Perigee, 2015), p. xxxiv.

5 Simon Sanek, *Start with Why: How great leaders inspire everyone to take action* (New York: Portfolio Penguin, 2009).

6 Andy Bounds, *The Snowball Effect: Communication techniques to make you unstoppable* (Chichester: Capstone, 2013).

7 Quoted in George Simmons, *Precalculus Mathematics in a Nutshell: Geometry, algebra, trigonometry* (Los Altos, CA: W. Kaufmann, 1981), p. 1.

8 Source unknown.

3 THE MESSAGE-TO-IDEA METAMORPHOSIS PRINCIPLE

1 Lucien Price, ed., *Dialogues of Alfred North Whitehead* (Boston: Little, Brown & Company, 1954), p. 100 (ch. 12, 28 April 1938).

2 Charles F. Brannan, US Secretary of Agriculture, from a broadcast over NBC, 3 April 1949.

3 Betty Birner, 'Does the Language I Speak Influence the Way I Think?', Linguistic Society of America: <http://www.linguistic society.org/content/does-language-i-speak-influence-way-i-think>.

4 Simon Hoggart, *House of Fun: 20 glorious years in Parliament* (London: Guardian Books, 2012), pp. 251–2.

5 Winston Churchill, in a speech made to the House of Commons, London, 13 May 1940.

6 From an introduction to the audio recording 'Churchill and World War Two', BBC Online, History section, World Wars (archived): <http://www.bbc.co.uk/history/worldwars/wwtwo/churchill_ audio_01.shtml>.

7 Winston Churchill, in a speech made to the House of Commons, London, 4 June 1940: <http://www.bbc.co.uk/history/worldwars/ wwtwo/churchill_audio_01.shtml>.

8 Quoted in Douglas Davis, *Creative Strategy and the Business of Design* (Blue Ash, OH: HOW Books, 2016), p. 133.

9 Science Direct, featuring research from the *Journal of Pragmatics* 41:4 (April 2009), pp. 699–720: <http://www.sciencedirect.com/ science/article/pii/S0378216608002798>.

10 Quoted in Robert G. Torricelli, ed., *Quotations for Public Speakers: A Historical, Literacy and Political Anthology* (New Brunswick, NJ: Rutgers University Press, 2001), p. 121.

11 German propaganda archive, Calvin College, Grand Rapids, MI: <http://research.calvin.edu/german-propaganda-archive/angrif13. htm>.

12 Translation of the original French: 'Les pierres du chantier ne sont en vrac qu'en apparence, s'il est, perdu dans le chantier, un homme, serait-il seul, qui pense cathédrale' – Antoine de Saint-Exupéry, *Pilote de guerre* (Paris: Gallimard, 1972 [orig. edn 1942]), p. 204.

13 Richard Branson: <https://www.virgin.com/node/108216>.

14 From the notebooks of Leonardo da Vinci; see <https://en.wiki source.org/wiki/The_Notebooks_of_Leonardo_Da_Vinci/XIX>.

4 THE WHY-FIRST PRINCIPLE

1 Kevin Roberts, *The Lovemarks Effect: Winning in the consumer revolution* (New York: PowerHouse Books, 2007), p. 35.

2 Fiona Kumfor, Sikong Tu, 'Can Your Brain Really Be "Full"?', *Scientific American*, 2 June 2015: <https://www.scientificamerican. com/article/can-your-brain-really-be-full/>.

3 Gladwell's entire book is built on this premise; see Malcolm Gladwell, *Outliers: The story of success* (New York: Little, Brown & Company, 2008). 'Deliberate practice' is a special type of focused practice conducted to improve performance.

5 THE CONTRASTING-OPTIONS PRINCIPLE

1 Bill Keller, 'Kevin Carter, a Pulitzer Winner for Sudan Photo, Is Dead at 33', *New York Times*, 29 July 1994.

2 Gary Wolf, 'Steve Jobs: The next insanely great thing', *Wired*, 2 January 1996.

3 Frank Barron, *Creative Person and Creative Process* (New York: Holt, Rinehart & Winston, 1969), pp. 132–3.

6 THE PICTURE-POWER PRINCIPLE

1 Carina Storrs, 'Sight Unseen: People blinded by brain damage can respond to emotive expressions', *Scientific American*, 14 October 2009; see <http://www.livescience.com/23709-blind-people-picture-reality.html>.

2 Jack Aspinwall, comp., *Tell Me Another! A new collection of after-dinner stories from the House of Lords and the House of Commons* (London: Century Hutchinson, 1986), p. 17.

3 'Researchers at Georgetown University Medical Center's Department of Neuroscience published their findings . . . in *The Journal of Neuroscience*. The paper, "Adding Words to the Brain's Visual Dictionary: Novel Word Selectively Sharpens Orthographic Representations in the VWFA", demonstrates the brain's ability to adapt and learn to recognize new words. The brain can add new words to its "visual dictionary" even if they are made up and have no meaning attached to them, the researchers found. In their previous work, the researchers had shown that the area in the left side of the visual cortex – roughly behind the left ear – seemed to have a visual dictionary that recognized whole words as images. The visual word form area (VWFA), as it's called, is opposite a similar brain area on the right side, called the fusiform face area (FFA), that quickly recognizes faces' – Stav Ziv, 'Your Brain Learns New Words as Pictures So You Can Read Faster', *Newsweek*, 25 March 2015. See also Karen Teber, 'After Learning New Words the Brain Sees Them as Pictures', 24 March 2015: <https://gumc.georgetown.edu/news/After-Learning-New-Words-Brain-Sees-Them-as-Pictures>.

4 Quoted in John Worne, 'Languages – Getting to the Heart', Center on Public Diplomacy, University of Southern California, 6 December 2013: <https://uscpublicdiplomacy.org/blog/languages-getting-hearts>.

5 Dr Lynell Burmark, Associate at the Thornburg Center for Professional Development and author of several books and papers on visual literacy, quoted in Karla Gutierrez, 'Studies Confirm the Power of Visuals in eLearning', Sh!ft: Disruptive eLearning, 8 July 2014: <http://info.shiftelearning.com/blog/bid/350326/Studies-Confirm-the-Power-of-Visuals-in-eLearning>.

6 Alister Doyle, 'Toasters Deadlier Than Sharks?', Reuters blog, 17 January 2008: <http://blogs.reuters.com/environment/2008/01/17/toasters-deadlier-than-sharks/>.

7 Walt Disney: <http://www.justdisney.com/walt_disney/quotes/index.html>.

8 Adam Withnall, 'Is This "160-Year-Old" Ethiopian Man the World's Oldest Ever Person?', *The Independent*, 13 September 2013.

9 Kevin Roberts, *Lovemarks: The future beyond brands* (New York: PowerHouse Books, 2006), p. 76.

10 Samuel M. McClure, Jian Li, Damon Tomlin, Kim S. Cypert, Latané M. Montague and P. Read Montague, 'Neural Correlates of Behavioral Preference for Culturally Familiar Drinks', *Neuron* 44:2 (14 October 2004), pp. 379–87.

11 Mike Parkinson (founder of Billion Dollar Graphics (BDG)), 'The Power of Visual Communication'; see <http://www.business2community.com/digital-marketing/visual-marketing-pictures-worth-60000-words-01126256#uLpITEuYbh66r30Y.97>.

12 Malcolm Gladwell, *Blink: The power of thinking without thinking* (New York: Little, Brown & Company, 2005), p. 12.

13 Andy Zubko, comp., *A Treasury of Spiritual Wisdom: A collection of 10,000 powerful quotations* (Delhi: Motilal Banarsidass, 2003), p. 338.

14 James Bigelow and Amy Poremba, 'Achilles' Ear? Inferior human short-term and recognition memory in the auditory modality', *PLOS ONE* 9:2 (2014): <http://journals.plos.org/plosone/article?id=10.1371/journal.pone.0089914>.

15 Source unknown.

16 From a translation of the original choreography and accompanying notes made by Julia Myles, the dance choreographer for the Salzburg 1998 performance, as part of the New English Orchestra.

7 THE EMOTIONAL-CONNECTION PRINCIPLE

1 Kevin Roberts, *The Lovemarks Effect: Winning in the consumer revolution* (New York: PowerHouse Books, 2007), p. 221.

2 Blaise Pascal, *De 'L'art de persuader* (On the Art of Persuasion) (written 1658, published posthumously).

3 Les Binet and Peter Field, *The Long and the Short of It: Balancing short and long-term marketing strategies* (London: IPA, 2013).

4 Charles Duhigg, 'What Google Learned from Its Quest to Build the Perfect Team', *New York Times* magazine, 25 February 2016: <http://www.nytimes.com/2016/02/28/magazine/what-google-learned-from-its-quest-to-build-the-perfect-team.html?_r=0>.

5 Kevin Roberts, *Lovemarks: The future beyond brands* (New York: PowerHouse Books, 2006), p. 76.

6 Email received from Gillian Colan-O'Leary, marketing consultant at Adoreboard, advertising a Webinar: 'Why Emotion Will Drive Your Customer Strategy in the Year Ahead', 2 December 2016.

7 Roberts, *Lovemarks Effect*, p. 35.

8 FIVE GREAT COMMUNICATORS

1 Joel Kleinman, 'Our Brains Are Made of the Same Stuff, Despite DNA Differences', National Institute of Health Study, 26 October 2011: <https://www.nih.gov/news-events/news-releases/our-brains-are-made-same-stuff-despite-dna-differences>.

2 'Creating New Neural Pathways in the Brain', *The Alternative Daily*: <http://www.thealternativedaily.com/creating-neural-path-brain/>.

3 Quoted by William Rees-Mogg in *The Times*, London, 4 April 2005.

4 Iain McGilchrist, *The Master and His Emissary: The divided brain and the making of the Western world* (New Haven, CT and London: Yale University Press, 2010).

5 Mark 4.30–31 (my emphasis).

6 John 8.7.

7 See Luke 10.25–37.

9 YOUR BODY'S NINTH SYSTEM: PERSUASION

1 Kevin Roberts, *The Lovemarks Effect: Winning in the consumer revolution* (New York: PowerHouse Books, 2007), p. 221.

2 Karene Booker, 'Scientists Discover How Brains Change with New Skills', *Cornell Chronicle*, 4 April 2013: <http://news.cornell.edu/stories/2013/04/scientists-discover-how-brains-change-new-skills>.

3 Mihaly Csikszentmihalyi, 'The Creative Personality', *Psychology Today*, 1 July 1996: <https://www.psychologytoday.com/articles/199607/the-creative-personality>.

4 Frank Barron, *Creativity and Psychological Health* (Princeton, NJ: D. Van Nostrand, 1963), p. 199.

10 A TECHNIQUE FOR FINDING IDEAS

1 Mary Potter is the senior author of the study. See Sarah Griffiths, 'Your Brain Really Is Faster Than You Think: It Takes Just 13 Milliseconds to See an Image, Scientists Discover', *Daily Mail*, 20 January 2014: <http://www.dailymail.co.uk/sciencetech/article-2542583/Scientists-record-fastest-time-human-image-takes-just-13-milliseconds.html>.

11 A TECHNIQUE FOR FINDING THE WHY

1 Nicholas Wright Gillham, *A Life of Sir Francis Galton: From African exploration to the birth of eugenics* (Oxford: Clarendon Press, 2001), p. 119.

13 A TECHNIQUE FOR EXTRACTING THE PICTURE

1 Hugh Jackman: <http://www.azquotes.com/quote/770385>.

14 A TECHNIQUE FOR GENERATING EMOTIONAL CONNECTION

1 Raphael Cushnir, 'Emotional Connection: Unleashing the Power of Emotional Connection', *Psychology Today*, 7 January 2009: <https://www.psychologytoday.com/blog/emotional-connection/200901/unleashing-the-power-emotional-connection>.

15 WHAT YOU PUT IN = WHAT YOU GET OUT

1 St Augustine: <http://www.orthodoxchurchquotes.com/category/sayings-from-saints-elders-and-fathers/st-augustine-of-hippo/>.